Contents

Acknowledgements

Immense thanks are due to all the members of the European Commission Network on Childcare (whose funding ended in 1996). The Network publications have been invaluable and are still the main source of reliable statistics on countries in the European Union.

Almost all the embassies of the EU countries sent some material for which I was grateful.

In terms of individuals, I would like to thank Kevin Kelman (previously at the Department of Child Care, Education and Health at the Glasgow College of Nautical Studies) for sharing the websites and other information he discovered in researching his European Perspectives course. Ann Robinson, Information Officer at the Early Childhood Unit, was as always a great source of help with written material of all kinds. I am grateful to Drew Lindon for help with the general background to the European Union and to Tanith Lindon for being my temporary research assistant for internet websites.

The photographs are from my collection – and thanks to Lance Lindon for taking some of them – with the exceptions on pages 83, 132 and 163 – with thanks to the Ullalinna School, Helsinki.

I accept the usual author's responsibility for outstanding mistakes and misunderstandings. With this book the possibility of confusion has been greater than ever, including the basic difficulty of identifying the difference between singular and plural in the many European languages that I do not speak. I have always tried to check two or more sources for the material but sometimes the genuine internal confusion about a country's early years services may emerge through that chapter. I would welcome suggestions, corrections and updates from readers that I will be pleased to integrate into revised editions.

Introduction

This book describes the childcare and educational systems within each of the fifteen countries that comprise the European Union. However, it is hard to make sense of the information without understanding the broader context of Europe. So, the book provides some general background in terms of geography, some history, economics and a sense of the peoples, cultures and languages that are represented in the continent.

Chapter 1 will help you to build a visual image of the countries of Europe and to understand the background to the European Union (EU): how it developed, the institutions of the EU and how the United Kingdom is involved. This chapter also provides a useful framework for understanding the value of a European perspective on early years provision, including how a cross-national view can support the understanding and development of our own national provision.

Chapter 2 extends this framework to cover some of the shared issues as well as differences between countries in the EU. The content will help you to understand the historical links between countries and their provision that are still relevant today. The UK shares many issues and concerns with other countries in the European Union. However, despite some elements of a shared European past, the fifteen EU countries are very different in their social, political and economic framework, let alone their early years and school services.

▶ **National background:** geographical location, politics and government, economic and social issues including language, population and urban-rural divisions.
▶ **Pre-school provision:** day care centres, family day care, the situation on family obligations and employment, early childhood education, any other early years provision.
▶ **Statutory education:** primary schooling and out-of-school provision.

1

Europe and the European Union

This book is about the childcare and educational systems within the countries that comprise the European Union. However, this first chapter will help you to place what happens within a broader context.

▶ The first section, 'Living in Europe', describes the variety within Europe and will help you build a visual image of the countries of the continent.
▶ The second section, 'Development of the European Union', explains the background to the European Union (EU): how it developed, the institutions of the EU and how the United Kingdom (UK) is involved.
▶ The third section, 'A European perspective on early years provision', provides a range of examples to highlight how a cross-national perspective can support the understanding and development of our own national provision.

Living in Europe

The continent of Europe

Europe is the second smallest of the world's continents and occupies nearly one-fifteenth of the world's total land area. The continent consists of the westward projecting peninsulas of the combined European and Asian land mass. However, Europe also includes many large and small islands.

Europe is mainly low-lying and even most of its mountain ranges are low compared with parts of South America or Asia. About three-fifths of the continent is less than 180 metres (600 feet) above sea level and another third lies between 180 and 900 metres (600 to 3000 feet). Some European countries, notably The Netherlands and the Fenland area of England, have reclaimed a high proportion of their land from the sea and consequently the population in these areas often live lower than sea level.

The fifteen countries comprising the EU

Variety in climate

The majority of Europe lies south of the Arctic Circle and north of the tropics and has a wide range of climates within the countries of the continent. Western Europe, which includes the UK, has a maritime climate. These countries are relatively close to the sea and its impact on the prevailing weather, so they have abundant rainfall and mild temperatures both in winter and summer. The western coastal parts of Europe, including the UK, have a mild climate despite being well north in the world because of the warming effects of the Gulf Stream. This warm oceanic current comes from the Atlantic Ocean and swirls around the coastlines.

The countries of central Europe have a transitional climate with rather less rainfall than the UK experiences but with relatively colder winters and warmer summers. North-eastern Europe has a continental climate with less rain again, long and cold winters and hot summers. The Mediterranean climate of southern coastal Europe has rainfall similar to the transitional climate areas but with mild, wet winters and hot, dry summers.

ACTIVITY: EUROPE IN CONTEXT

Look at the map on page 2 as you read this section and add to your current understanding of Europe.

▶ **Get to know the locations of the different countries in relationship to the UK and each other. We are used to having coastal borders but other EU countries have land borders with several other nations and some are completely landlocked.**

▶ **Check out those European countries that you have visited, either on holiday or for work or student exchanges. Get a clearer sense of their location in relation to other countries in the continent.**

▶ **You can see that the coastline of mainland Europe is very irregular. There are a considerable number of bays, fjords and seas within the continent, so that the total coastline is close to 38 000 kilometres (24 000 miles) in length.**

▶ **Prior to the building of the channel tunnel, leaving the UK other than by aeroplane meant planning to cross one of the seas that surrounds us. However, everyday life in some other European countries, for instance Denmark or the many islands that comprise Greece, involves crossing a stretch of water.**

▶ **Unless you travel well up the few higher mountains in Europe, for instance in Austria or Switzerland, you will never find out whether** you suffer from altitude sickness, because you will never be high enough above sea level. In other parts of the world, some of them with sizeable populations, for instance Colorado in the United States, daily life is lived at a higher altitude (6000 feet) than can be found even on the highest UK mountain.

▶ Look at a world map and draw a line across westwards from Europe. You will see that even southern England is on the same latitude as Canada, which has seriously harsh winters. We are protected by the Gulf Stream.

The population

The people of Europe constitute about one-seventh of the total world population and the continent is the second most densely populated continent after Asia. The area of highest population density stretches from England, across northern France to the Rhine-Ruhr area of Germany and southward to northern Italy. In terms of total population in 1998, the EU countries vary from Germany with the largest at 82.3 million to Luxembourg with the smallest at 0.4 million.

CHILDREN IN THE POPULATION

Europe has the lowest rate of natural increase of population for any continent. Despite low mortality rates and good general health, the fertility rates are so low in some western and central European countries that the net population growth is at or near zero, meaning that just about as many babies are born as there are people dying. The overall population level in some countries is only maintained through immigration.

Fertility rates are calculated in different ways but a usual method is to link the birth rate to the population of women of child-bearing age. So the fertility rates quoted in this section are for births per every 1000 women of child-bearing age in that country.

The fertility rate has been generally falling in Europe during the second half of the twentieth century. In 1992 the fertility rates in EU countries (then twelve in total) averaged at 1.48 and any country needs a rate of 2.1 just to replace the population. In Italy, Germany and Spain the fertility rate was 1.3. or lower. From the 1960s to the 1990s the average fertility rate in European countries fell by about 30%, the average rate in the 1960s being closer to 2.67. Only the three Scandinavian EU countries and Luxembourg have rising fertility rates in the final decades of the twentieth century.

Consequently, the proportion of the total population under fifteen years in EU countries has generally been declining. In 1998 the proportion of under fifteens varied from 15% in Italy to 23% in Ireland. However, in 1950 EU countries generally had higher proportions of children in the population, for instance, the UK with 22%, Italy and Denmark with about 26% and Ireland with nearly 29%. The falling child population has been most noticeable in Ireland and southern EU countries like Spain.

URBAN LIVING

The population of Europe mainly lives in urban areas with this trend being most marked in those countries with a high level of industrialisation. So, the UK and Germany are among the European countries with the most urbanised population and Albania (non-EU) and Portugal are the least.

This strong tendency for the population to live in towns and cities can shape national policy around the assumption that people live in urban areas. Consequently, in the UK, as in some other EU countries, there has to be a concerted effort to get rural issues onto the agenda. Urban based planners and policy makers have to understand that the way services work in towns and cities is often not directly transferable to more rural areas of the country.

Languages and cultural background

Europe has many divisions of nationality and language. The reasons for the diversity are that the continent has been inhabited for a very long time and the ethnic groups within the area have tended not to be very mobile. Europe has about 60 languages that are indigenous to the continent. Most of these fall into three main language divisions all of which derive from an original Indo-European language that appears to have been brought to the continent many centuries ago by migrants from south-western Asia. There are three main groupings.

▶ **The Romance languages** originated with Latin and include French, Spanish, Portuguese, Italian, Romanian and Romansch.
▶ **The Germanic languages** are derived from a common language of ancient peoples in southern Scandinavia and Denmark. This group includes German, English, Netherlandic (Dutch and Flemish), Danish, Norwegian, Swedish and Icelandic.
▶ **The Slavic language** group is concentrated in eastern and south-eastern Europe and includes Russian, Polish, Czech, Slovak, Ukrainian, Belorussian, Bulgarian, Slovene and Serbo-Croatian.

The remaining indigenous European languages do not fit any of the above three groupings. Greek is a language of Indo-European origin. Hungarian and Finnish have more in common with each other than with other European languages and are called **Finno–Ugric languages**. In southern Europe a range of **Turkic languages** are spoken.

There is also a group of **Celtic languages**, a sub-group also of Indo-European origin, that includes Welsh, Scottish and Irish Gaelic and Breton. Some languages from this group now only survive in a written form, for instance Manx Gaelic or Cornish.

Cultural and religious diversity

The separate national and linguistic groups developed their own cultural traditions, supported by distinctive styles of national dress (less obvious now except on special occasions) and creative arts and music.

The religious background to culture in Europe is overwhelmingly Christian. However, historically there have been such divisions that religious belief has rarely brought a sense of unity between countries that follow a different branch within the three main divisions: Catholic, Protestant and Eastern Orthodox Christian churches. Some longstanding Muslim communities are also scattered through Europe.

Other languages, religions and cultural traditions have arrived in Europe through population movements from other parts of the world, especially during the second part of the twentieth century. Some of these immigrants came out of choice for economic reasons, seeking employment and better prospects than in their country of origin. Some people came from former colonies of European countries, established during the time of imperialist expansion in the nineteenth and early twentieth centuries into Africa, Asia and the Far East.

Other population movements have been as the result of war and political upheaval in parts of Europe itself or other continents of the world. The refugee movements from the upheaval in the former Yugoslavia are only the most recent of the refugee crises of the twentieth century.

National borders

It is important to realise that some of the national boundaries on the map of Europe are much less than even a century old. The defining borders of some countries have a long history, whereas others were only determined within the twentieth century, many as a consequence of the disruption following the end of the First World War in 1918 and the Second World War in 1945.

Politically convenient boundaries often cut across diverse national and cultural identities and subsequent events have led to the break-up of some countries. The end of the former Soviet Union (part of the continents of Europe and Asia) and political breakdown in the former Yugoslavia has led to war, civil disruption and the determination of new national boundaries. The map of Europe is by no means fixed.

The few nomadic peoples of Europe, for instance the Sami (known to outsiders as the Lapp) in northern Scandinavia, have traditional homelands that span several countries (see also page 79).

Economic systems

Europe was the first of the major regions of the world to develop a modern economy based on commercial agriculture and industrial development. The continent as a whole remains one of the world's major industrial regions with an average income per head that is among one of the highest in the world. Europe accounts for about half of the world's international trade. The countries of Western Europe are among the world's most well-off, but the southern and eastern parts of the continent are noticeably less prosperous. There are significant areas of poverty and deprivation within some of the more economically successful European countries, including the UK.

The western, democratically run countries of Europe have been oriented to the economic markets, with varying degrees of government intervention. The communist governments in the previous Soviet Union and non-EU countries such as Poland and Romania, that were part of the soviet bloc, used to run economies that were highly planned and controlled through central government. From 1989 to 1991 the Soviet Union lost control of eastern Europe and the communist governments of the region steadily collapsed. Political change has led to economies that are more responsive to the market, as opposed to high government control of demand and supply. There has also been a growth of new consumer goods and service industries. The pattern of daily life in such countries has changed considerably.

Diversity in political systems

The political systems within Europe differ. All have central governments but the precise role and responsibilities differ.

- ▶ Some countries have most authority resting with the central government and its different departments. But even some of the most longstanding centralised systems are attempting some level of decentralisation, for instance Greece.
- ▶ Some countries, such as Denmark, have decentralised power so that the different regions of the country make most of the decisions relevant to local services and events.
- ▶ A federal system, as in Germany and Austria, involves the union of several distinct regions or states under a central government in such a way that each state retains control of its internal affairs. The country forms a political unity and is represented as a single nation in foreign affairs. However, defined local areas retain full responsibility and control for their internal affairs in the region. The overall federal government may pass legislation but the regions still retain some level of independence in running services within the legislative framework.
- ▶ Other European countries are in a state of change through intended decentralisation or because of other changes in the structure of the country, for instance the UK and the impact of devolution of power to Wales and Scotland.
- ▶ Seven EU countries have a constitutional monarchy: Belgium, Denmark, Luxembourg, The Netherlands, Sweden and the UK have retained their monarchy and Spain reinstated the royal family. The current king or queen acts as the official head of state and may confirm acts of parliament but has limited real power.
- ▶ Some EU countries have retained relatively stable democratic systems. However, others have experienced high levels of political instability (Italy and Portugal) and authoritarian governments (Portugal, Greece, Italy and Spain) within the life span of the current adult population.

Development of the European Union

Summary

THE GROWTH OF EU MEMBERSHIP

The following section describes the development of what is now known as the European Union. This box summarises the entry point of each country, into what at the time was sometimes known by a different name:

▶ **1958:** France, Germany (at that point only West Germany) Italy, Luxembourg, Belgium and The Netherlands.
▶ **1973:** UK, Denmark and Ireland
▶ **1981:** Greece
▶ **1986:** Portugal and Spain
▶ **1990:** East Germany entered as part of a reunified Germany
▶ **1995:** Austria, Finland and Sweden.

The beginning of European unity

THE 1950s

The body that is now called the European Union (EU) started through the efforts of six European countries: France, Germany (at that point West Germany, known as the Federal Republic of Germany) Italy, Luxembourg, Belgium and The Netherlands.

At the end of the Second World War the economies of European countries were in a dire state. This group of six countries worked together with a vision of a peaceful and cooperative Europe in the future and with a strong motivation to rebuild the economy. In 1952 the six governments formed the European Coal and Steel Community (ECSC). This development created a free trade area for coal and steel that were at that time crucial industries for Europe. In 1957 the same countries formed the European Atomic Energy Authority (EAEC) to encourage the growth of peaceful uses of nuclear power. By the time this treaty was complete, negotiations were also under way for an even more ambitious form of unity in Europe.

The European Economic Community (EEC), also known as the Common Market, came into existence in 1958, following the signing by member countries of the Treaty of Rome the previous year. The treaty established a customs union with the aim that all tariffs between the countries would eventually be removed and this was completed by 1986. The Treaty of Rome also included provisions that in the future there should be a free flow not just of goods between the countries but also of money and of people being able to move around to seek work.

THE 1960s

With the aim of creating a more harmonious and coherent Europe, the Treaty also envisaged the later creation of a number of common policies for member countries. The Common Agricultural Policy was established in 1962 and regional, transport and social policy followed. Some areas of policy have met with more national resistance than others. The Treaty of Rome also created four important institutions which still exist in the same way today and in some instances with growing power. These are the European Commission, Council of Ministers, Parliament and Court of Justice (more on page 12).

For some years the pre-existing European bodies continued alongside the EEC but in 1967 the ECSC and the EAEC become one with the Community and the whole organisation became the European Economic Communities (EEC, the plural was dropped from the name in the 1980s).

The UK and Europe

The UK decided not to join the EEC in 1958. Government policy makers were convinced at that time that the Community would not emerge as a significant European body. There was also a strong preference to retain links with the United States and with colonies and former colonies within the British Commonwealth.

As an alternative European organisation, in 1960 the UK helped to form the European Free Trade Association (EFTA) with Austria, Denmark, Norway, Portugal, Sweden and Switzerland. Finland also joined slightly later. EFTA was a free trade association rather than a customs union and had no vision of developing into a more active European state.

The UK swiftly decided that a wrong decision had been made to opt for EFTA membership and in 1962 applied to join the EEC. The application was persistently blocked by France, concerned about losing the dominance they enjoyed with Germany. This situation continued for over ten years until the UK was finally successful in 1973. Denmark and Ireland also joined in the same year. At this time Greenland was a dependent state under Danish rule. However, when Greenland became separate from Denmark, they chose to withdraw from the EEC in 1985.

Development from the 1970s

During the 1970s attempts were made to move the EEC toward a single European currency. In 1979 the framework of the European Monetary System (EMS) was established to regulate currency exchange rates and to support monetary stability among member countries. The UK, Portugal and Spain refused to become a part of the EMS. The currencies of the majority of the EEC countries were linked so as to avoid large day-by-day fluctuations. At the same time, restrictions on the movement of labour among the EEC countries was also removed to encourage mobility.

With the addition of Greece in 1981 and Spain and Portugal in 1986, the political balance of the EEC had shifted somewhat and increased the relative importance of agriculture in the Community. The Single European Act came into force in 1987 and committed governments to the removal of other remaining trade barriers. The awareness that the EEC was no longer focussed just on economic issues led to a change of name to the European Community (EC).

THE MAASTRICHT TREATY

The success of earlier trade policies made member countries more receptive to a greater economic and political integration within Europe. In 1989 the European Commission put forward proposals for a Social Charter to guarantee the rights of workers across the Community and this became the Social Chapter of the Treaty on European Union (commonly known as the Maastricht Treaty) in 1992.

The Treaty laid down the timetable for the single European currency and established a structure for cooperation in foreign policy between member countries. To recognise the further change in the nature of the European cooperation the name was changed to the European Union (EU). The Maastricht Treaty established a European Monetary Institute and by 1994 had created a vast free trade zone, the European Economic Area (EEA), between EU members and EFTA members Norway and Iceland, but not Switzerland and Liechtenstein.

From 1990 measures were implemented to move member countries towards a unified market with the lifting of exchange controls and the removal of barriers to Europe-wide financial services like banking and insurance. By the end of the 1990s the international European currency of the euro was established. All national currencies still remain, and the euro is given in some EU countries in price lists as well as the national currency.

New and potential members in the 1990s

The former East Germany (the German Democratic Republic) was admitted to the EU as part of a reunified Germany in 1990 (see page 99). In 1995 Austria, Finland and Sweden left EFTA and became members of the EU. By the mid-1990s several other countries were interested in joining the EU, including Poland and Hungary (Eastern European countries that had been in the Communist bloc), Albania and Slovenia (Southern European countries) and Turkey (most of which is geographically in Asia).

The existing member countries are concerned about a very unwieldy EU if the membership continues to expand. There is also concern that some of the interested countries would be net recipients of EU money, so countries whose economic condition would make them net contributors are wary about the cost to themselves. The countries awaiting a decision on membership have more rural based economies than the balance in the existing EU and so are unlikely to have the same priorities as current members.

A date of 2003 has been set for six of the eleven waiting countries to join the EU. It is possible that a range of membership or association options might be developed. A possible pattern already exists in the relationship between the EU and the remaining countries of EFTA, with the exception of Switzerland and Liechtenstein.

The regulatory and legal framework of the EU

The Treaty of Rome created several controlling bodies for what was then the EEC. Under the European Union, these bodies are still central and in some ways more powerful. These institutions may seem remote from the UK and the topic of this book. However, their actions continue to exert an impact on our own early years services and the supporting framework. Specific examples are given in this section.

THE EUROPEAN COMMISSION

The Commission is based in Brussels (Belgium) and is effectively the civil service of the EU. The Commission has ten members, a president and six vice-presidents who are selected by member countries.

The commission is responsible for the implementation of the different treaties of the EU and the various rules issued by the Council of Ministers (see page 13). As well as being responsible for current policy and practice, the Commission also helps to prepare new Acts to be submitted to the European Parliament and the Council. So, the Commission does not have the power simply to take through all the changes that it initiates. Proposals are made, Parliament and Council make decisions and the Commission then implements proposals that have been passed.

The Commission's Equal Opportunities Unit has funded projects and reviews that are of direct relevance to early years services in the UK and to the topic of this book. The Maastricht Treaty (see page 11) established that the role of the EU was not just economic. The Treaty established a social role for the EU: to aim for a balanced development of economic activities, to allow for social protection issues, raising standards of living and the quality of life.

The European Commission entered the arena of early years services through a series of action programmes on the Promotion of Equal Opportunities for Women, the First Programme from 1982–5. The Commission funded the European Commission Network on Childcare (more on page 34) as part of the second action programme (1986–90). This Network was set up and funded from 1986–96 to have an expert from each member state and a co-ordinator (Peter Moss of the Thomas Coram Research Unit in London). The Childcare Network was one of several Equality Networks funded by the Commission's Equal Opportunities Unit (within the Commission's Directorate-General V on Employment, Industrial Relations and Social Affairs). The Network's role was to monitor developments, evaluate policy options and collect and disseminate information.

Within the third action programme (1991–5) the Commission set up the Community Initiative Programme which included the New Opportunities for Women (NOW) which was the first EU programme specifically to allocate funding to the development of services for young children.

THE COUNCIL OF MINISTERS OF THE EUROPEAN UNION

The Council has the power either to approve or reject new policies proposed by the Commission. Depending on the topic, the relevant Minister, for instance, agriculture or finance, from each member country is present for the discussion and decisions. So, every member country has a representative in any discussion.

Although the Council is obliged to consult the European Parliament on various legislative matters, it still wields real power of decision within the

EU. It determines how treaties are to be carried out and what exactly is the intent of details of any treaty. The Council also determines how the national policies, for instance economic, of member countries have to be coordinated to achieve the aims of EU treaties.

In 1992 the Council adopted a Recommendation on Childcare, which was a political commitment from all the member states (twelve at the time) to various aspects of early years policy. Recommendations do not carry the legal force of an EU Directive but nevertheless are expected to lead to national action.

The main purpose of the Recommendation was to encourage member states to review their childcare services with the objective 'to encourage initiatives to enable women and men to reconcile their occupational, family and upbringing responsibilities arising from the care of children' (Article 1). The Recommendation proposed the need for initiatives in four areas:

1 Childcare services without which employed parents could not be involved in the labour market (Article 3).
2 Leave for employed parents that would ease the reconciliation of work and family responsibilities (Article 4).
3 The workplace environment, structure and organisation, in order to make it more responsive to the needs of workers with children (Article 5).
4 Measures to promote the increased participation of men in the care and upbringing of children and to lead to a more equal sharing of responsibility between men and women to enable women to have a more effective role in the labour market (Article 6).

The European Parliament

The Parliament is the legislative assembly of the EU and meets either in Brussels (Belgium) or in Strasbourg (France). The Parliament consists of elected representatives (Members of the European Parliament, MEPs) from each member country. Elections for MEPs are held and you can vote in the usual way.

The Parliament was historically relatively weak and tended in the early years simply to make official a series of decisions that had been completed elsewhere in the EU structure. The Treaty of Maastricht increased the powers of the Parliament and it is the intention that the European Parliament will over time become stronger, acting more like an international parliament for Europe. The Parliament has specialised standing committees on the different topics relevant to Europe, such as social affairs and employment or energy and research.

THE EUROPEAN COURT OF JUSTICE

The Court is the judicial branch of the EU and meets in Luxembourg City. The full Court consists of thirteen judges and six advocates-general who are appointed by member governments. The Court reviews the legality of what is done by the Commission and the Council. This body is also the ultimate court of law for the European Union and generally deals with disputes between member countries over trade or environmental issues.

The Court is additionally responsible for making judgements on EU law, including whether the laws of member countries contravene Union law. The Court is the final arbiter on the growing body on international law that has developed with the economic and political integration within Europe. The Court has the right to invalidate the national laws of member countries if they conflict with EU law. The Court regularly passes judgements that have implications obligating member countries to make national changes. For instance, the judgement on equal pension rights for women and men in 1992 forced the UK government to develop plans to equalise the state retirement age for men and women at 65 years.

Member countries can be taken before the European Court if they fail to follow obligations arising from EU law. Italy has most cases held against it in the Court, a total of 355. In contrast, the UK has had 45 cases held against it and Denmark even less.

The Court also has the power to hear issues raised by private parties and deal with compensation for damages. Individuals in any member country can appeal to the Court when they feel they have exhausted the legal possibilities in their own country and have not obtained justice. For instance, in September 1998, the Court found that the repeated caning of a young boy by his stepfather breached Article 3 of the European Human Rights Convention and that current UK law had therefore failed to give this child adequate protection and should be changed.

ACTIVITY: NEWS REPORT WITH A EUROPEAN FLAVOUR

Over a period of a few weeks, keep cuttings of any news items or features that have a European perspective, especially anything relevant to children and families. Look over your collection and get a sense of the overall feel (positive or negative) and the ways in which the topics could be relevant to early years provision as you experience it.

A European perspective on early years provision

The United Kingdom has been geographically part of Europe for a long time, but joining the European Union brought the UK into a different European identity.

Learning from other countries

The media of television and newspapers tend to focus on the economic consequences of the EU as well as the alleged interfering presumption of some directives from Brussels. Yet, within early years care and education and playwork there have been a growing number of positive cross-national contacts since the 1980s and with increasing frequency through the 1990s.

Joint projects, networks or forums have resulted in professional discussion, some publications and international conferences. These group and individual contacts have represented a strong wish to learn from other countries, especially fellow European countries. More widespread use of e-mail and internet websites has eased the task of communicating with interested parties who work hundreds of miles apart. Some international networks are listed on page 196.

Without an understanding of other countries, it is so easy to assume that your own national pattern of early years values and services is the usual or best possible system. Undoubtedly some caution needs to be taken in understanding what kind of provision is actually meant in different countries by general terms like **'creche'** or **'kindergarten'**, since national systems vary considerably. The different ways of collecting, or not gathering, statistics on different kinds of provision can also make cross-national

The Bridgwater Forest School – an example of cross-national contact

comparisons difficult (see the example on page 40). However, if you bear some of the practical issues in mind, there is much to learn from different systems and a few general examples follow.

HOW MUCH DIVERSITY?

Without an international perspective, it can seem that the many different types of early years provision in the UK are what will inevitably develop in any European country. In fact, the UK system of childcare and education appears very diverse and fragmented when compared with the systems of some other EU countries. The diversity may sometimes be presented politically as a positive choice for families, but in reality there may be little choice in many areas.

Some voluntary forms of provision, such as the playgroup movement, may seem like a specifically UK response. Yet, in a number of EU countries, playgroups have developed as an established facility for children under the age for statutory schooling but usually at least two to three years old. As well as the UK (see page 186), The Netherlands (page 148), Ireland (page 124) and Finland (page 84) all have strong, although slightly different, playgroup movements. Finland's playgroups were established by the Lutheran Church after the second world war, but the other national developments were started during the 1960s as an alternative to existing provision and to fill a gap in services for children and their families.

IS CHILDCARE A PRIVATE FAMILY ISSUE?

Increased knowledge about other national systems can help you to reflect on the underpinning values and assumptions in your own early years provision. For instance, the UK shares with some other EU countries the conviction that day care, in contrast with pre-school education, is a form of provision necessitated by maternal employment and therefore a private family matter.

However, some EU countries, for instance Denmark, have an integrated system in which all the services for young children are viewed as provision for young citizens. The EU Nordic countries as a whole (Sweden, Denmark and Finland) are unusual in the EU in that they have provision for children under three years that is mainly available through publicly funded services rather than privately run provision.

SHOULD CHILDCARE PROVISION BE SEPARATE FROM EARLY EDUCATION?

Again, the assumption has been in the UK that services for day care of young children are different from, and often seen as the poor relation of, nursery education. Although some EU countries share the care-education split that bedevils a coherent UK system, other countries have (Denmark) or are working towards (Spain) a genuine early years service that recognises the needs of children for both care and learning, often called an educare approach.

DIFFERENT VALUES OR PERCEIVED PROBLEMS

Cross-national contact can also throw new light on what are believed to be the key issues in an area of practice. Early years workers are predominantly female and all EU countries have at least some wish to bring in more males. However views differ about the issues involved.

A 1997 conference on men as workers in services for children brought together practitioners and researchers from the UK with those from Denmark, Finland, Norway and Sweden. Discussion soon highlighted the mutual confusion and disagreement between the UK and other delegates.

The UK group saw child protection issues as central and problematic to bringing more men into early years. In contrast, the Nordic delegates felt strongly that the UK, in common with the United States, has developed a seriously unbalanced view, bordering on obsession, with the risk of child abuse and male workers. The Nordic group considered child protection as an issue in early years, but saw the need to increase numbers of male workers as part of gender equality for adults and appropriate gender learning for children. (The papers from the conference are published in Owen, Cameron and Moss, 1998, full reference on page 194.)

CROSS-NATIONAL SUPPORT FOR CHANGE

The experience of one country can suggest the possibility of change for another, even allowing that laws, provision and the social context are very different.

The UK based alliance called 'Children are unbeatable' aims to change the law in England and Wales to give children the same rights against physical assault as adults. The alliance is able to draw on the experience of other European countries that have legally banned all forms of corporal punishment of children.

Austria, Denmark, Finland and Sweden (EU countries), Croatia, Cyprus, Latvia and Norway (non-EU members) have all changed the national law. Sweden was the first country in the world to ban corporal punishment of children on a national basis in 1979. Research material from different countries, especially from the twenty years of Swedish experience since the ban, offer the alliance a firm basis for refuting some of the claims of groups in favour of hitting children.

In a different example, the UK campaign for home zones, led by the Children's Play Council, aims to create safe neighbourhood areas for children and local people that are more friendly towards pedestrians and less oriented to cars. The organisation Pressure Group 2000 has contributed to the ideas by visiting similar home zones operating in The Netherlands and exploring how zones are already operational in Austria, Denmark and Sweden. Under current UK legislation it is not possible for local authorities to give priority to pedestrians over cars, but the cross-national experience gives a useful perspective on what can work.

SCHOOL EXPERIENCE

Cross-national information can also give an alternative perspective on a national form of provision undergoing planned or unplanned change.

The statutory age for starting school in England, Wales and Scotland remains five years. However, since the 1970s increasing numbers of four year olds have been admitted to the reception classes of primary schools. This process was accentuated by many local authorities in the 1990s who have offered allegedly 'pre-school places' to four year olds but made them available in primary schools and not in the more appropriate provision of nursery classes or schools. The prevailing official argument that early entry must be better has been challenged by early years professionals not only from a national basis but also from a broader European perspective. The UK is in a minority in the EU in starting children so young (see also page 35) and research suggests that later starts to formal education do not disadvantage children. In fact children's later achievements are sometimes improved.

Comparison between EU countries also highlights the varied national patterns for school opening hours and terms. The assumption of anyone who has experienced the UK system will be that of a school day lasting into the mid-afternoon, of a supervised lunch break and the provision of school dinners (not always a happy memory!) or somewhere to eat a packed lunch. However, many EU countries run a school day that finishes at lunchtime or soon afterwards. Until recently, children in some countries were expected to go home for the lunch break, which might be as long as three hours in southern European countries where an afternoon siesta is normal. Hours vary between the days of the week and some have Saturday school. The pattern of school holidays can be very different between EU countries, some having up to six holiday blocks and not all with the long summer holiday known in the UK.

The benefits of professional contact

An increasing number of early years practitioners seek the opportunity to visit other European contexts. Colleges who offer courses relevant to early years care and education wish to build in some European perspective, even though this will not always be an entire course or unit. Some colleges organise trips or exchanges for students to visit other EU countries. The three main advantages are to:

1 Learn about other systems and gain a sense of perspective on our own.
2 Listen to the perspectives of visitors to our own UK systems and to consider their reactions to what seems normal to us.
3 Consider provision that seems innovatory to us and how we may be able to use the ideas in our own context.

Cross-national contacts can provide access to new ideas in practice, either that are normal within a given country or are unusual for that national system.

You have to be cautious in making sense of any provision that is visited. Innovatory or trailblazer projects may not be typical of the country as a whole, as indeed poor practice may not be typical either. It is unsafe to make national generalisations until you have a reasonable level of understanding about a particular national system. For instance, there is continued interest in the UK in the Reggio Emilia early years system that is established in a part of northern Italy (see page 132). However, this approach to early years is not typical of the rest of Italy's day care and early education and is a development particular to this region.

It is also unlikely that ideas, however good, can simply be copied between countries; the social context will be different. However, a different kind of provision working well in another country can raise the possibility that this idea might work for your own area.

EXAMPLES OF CROSS-NATIONAL CONTACTS

▶ **One**

A Swedish pedagogue, Gunilla Dahlberg, described her experience and reflection on visiting a pre-school in the Reggio Emilia region of Italy. She was surprised and rather shocked to see an array of commercialised playthings in the pre-school – including He-Man toys and My Little Pony – which were discouraged in the Swedish settings in favour of wooden play materials. In discussion with the Italian team, Dahlberg discovered that they had focussed on how important such play figures were to the children and had realised that they, as adults, undervalued and dismissed the toys.

The Italian team had set about personal research through watching the relevant television programmes and really listening to what the children had to say. They came to recognise the importance to the children, the detail of their interest and pretend play. Consequently the Italian team, in a way that is typical of the regional approach to children, had started a project with the children on modern fairy tale figures, being guided by the children's own experiences, ideas and stories. (A short descriptive report is given in Dahlberg, Moss and Pence, full reference on page 194.)

▶ **Two**

From the mid-1980s staff and student exchanges have been taking place between the Oxford Polytechnic Early Childhood Centre and the **Högskalen I Örebro** in Sweden. Students from each country have reacted with both positive comments and some reservations about the other country's system. (Reported in *Early Years*, vol 12, no 2, 1992.)

▶ **Three**

The Early Childhood Centre at the Roehampton Institute in London has links with colleagues in Denmark, Portugal and Sweden. There are funds for student exchange and the development of ideas about the early years curriculum. (One student's visit to Denmark was reported in *Early Years*, vol 14, no1, 1993.)

▶ **Four**

In 1995 a group of Nursery Nursing students from Bridgwater College (Somerset, England) visited the Forest School provision in Denmark (see page 71). The enthusiasm of the group led to a similar facility which has been developed by a team from the Bridgwater College and Early Excellence Centre. That team has worked over a matter of years to develop the Danish concept in a way that makes sense within the UK traditions and values. (There is a report in *Nursery World*, 16 January 1997 or contact the Information Officer at the Centre on 01278 455464.)

▶ **Five**

During the mid-1990s, an English nursery school linked up via the internet with an Italian **scuole materne** and a French **école maternelle**. The

English team gained funding from the UK Central Bureau for Educational Visits and Exchanges. The children have enjoyed a detailed exchange of e-mails, photographs and videos of their respective settings, drawings and paintings. (Reported in *Early Education*, Summer 1999.)

▶ **Six**

In 1998 a group of students from Redcar and Cleveland College (Yorkshire, England) visited Rome. The group were completing the BTEC module on Childcare in Europe and the college had arranged an exchange between the English and Italian students. The English students created a website to report on their visit. The account is suitably cautious about national generalisations from visits to a few city settings. However, the students were able to reflect on some variations between the Italian settings and UK experience, including differences in curriculum approach and to safety issues. You can access the website on
http://www.cleveland.ac.uk/exchange/italians/italy.htm

▶ **Seven**

In 1999 a group of students on the Childcare course at Glasgow College of Nautical Studies visited Madrid. The group was able to see a range of provision in the Spanish capital city for under threes and three to six year-olds in a system that has the political aim of merging care and education, but has not yet managed to implement the development. The group was interested in a number of issues, including the communication with parents through a notelet that formed the end of day contact with parents of very young children. The students were also struck that the Madrid workers reached a different balance between safety and allowing children to explore minor risk than they would themselves have expected in Scotland. The group returned with food for thought. (*Source*: personal communication from Kevin Kelman, Glasgow College of Nautical Studies.)

▶ **Eight**

The training systems of some other EU countries have a cross-national link as an integral part of the student experience. For example, the Stockholm Institute of Education, the largest training institute for teachers in Sweden, has the four-year International Programme in Early Childhood Education in which one year is spent elsewhere as part of an EU exchange programme. The integral early years qualification of paedagoger in Denmark also includes a work placement in another EU country.

ACTIVITY: REPORTS OF CROSS NATIONAL CONTACT

Keep an alert eye for reports of cross-national contacts between different early years professionals or student groups. Exchange visits and innovatory provision inspired by other national systems are often reported in practical magazines such as *Nursery World*.

Look out for any opportunities that you may have through your college, any local early years network or by becoming adept at internet contacts.

2

Children and families in the European Union

This chapter covers some of the shared issues as well as differences between countries in the EU. Chapters 3 to 17 cover each individual country and you should use this chapter to gain a framework for making sense of what happens in the different countries.

A shared European past

Industrialisation and the need for childcare

European countries share a historical pattern that day care for children arose from increased industrialisation and the employment of women in the new factories. Different countries faced the impact of industrialisation at varied points within the nineteenth and twentieth centuries. The accompanying social change was one of significant population shifts from the countryside into the towns and cities. The UK experienced a relatively early industrialisation at the beginning of the nineteenth century, whereas countries such as Greece did not develop day care in response to industrialisation until the end of the same century.

Day nurseries were privately rather than state run and aimed only at the children of the working classes. The upper classes dealt with their childcare needs through employing nannies and child nurses. The aim of the day nurseries was to supervise the children and to instil some principles of hygiene and moral education. Some of these private developments were positive for children, especially in the context of their time, for example, the nurseries developed by Robert Owen in England in the early 1800s (see page 27).

Some forms of day care came to be influenced by the early educational models proposed by a number of influential thinkers (see page 26). Other day care settings remained supervisory in nature and were viewed as institutions forced to exist because of maternal employment. The negative traditions associated with care in contrast with early education have persisted for decades in many EU countries.

Traditions of early childhood education

In Europe the concept of early childhood education followed later than any provision of childcare for working mothers. The developments in early education were generally separate from any ideas of day care and the hours of the services were never designed to fit adult working hours. Early childhood education was also usually seen as appropriate for the second half of early childhood, usually for children over three years of age – a division that persists in the systems of several EU countries.

From the middle of the nineteenth century, European countries began to introduce legislation specifically about education prior to the statutory school age for children. The first countries to develop legislation were France in 1837 and Spain in 1857. Of the current EU countries, the UK was one of the later group, (legislation relating to pre-school education was passed from 1944–47). Ireland was the last and did not have any statutory reference to pre-school children until 1991, having long admitted four year-olds to infant schools.

A number of key thinkers and innovators influenced several, sometimes many, of the developing European systems for children. Although their ideas and practice differed, they shared a commitment to a child-centred approach. In practice this meant a conviction that early educational establishments should be fitted to the needs of children, rather than children be forced into practices that are convenient for schools. Some key names within Europe include the following individuals, who are given in chronological order.

JOHANN PESTALOZZI (1746–1827)

Pestalozzi was a Swiss educational reformer. He was influenced by the ideas of the French philosopher-educator, Jean-Jacques Rousseau and developed a very radical educational approach for the time.

Pestalozzi stressed that instruction of children should start with the familiar and move on to new ideas. Any programme should be paced to follow the gradual unfolding of a child's development. His curriculum focussed on activities in which children worked together as they steadily learned how to think. The underlying principle was that children were enabled to move from observation to comprehension and then to the formation of ideas. Pestalozzi was unable to put his ideas into practice until he was more than fifty years old and his Yverdon Institute ceased to function towards the end of his life. However, his ideas have been very influential because of their impact on Froebel.

ROBERT OWEN (1771–1858)

Owen was a Welshman who owned a textile factory in New Lanark in Scotland. He was a successful businessman who also had a passionate concern for the well being of his workforce and their children. In 1819 he opened the first infant school in Britain at his mills.

Owen's educational philosophy was based in his conviction that the early years of childhood were a vital time to develop health and a positive character in children. Such a view may seem normal now but was very unusual in Owen's time when prevailing Christian religious beliefs focussed far more on the allegedly sinful nature of young children. Although Owen's name is not as well known as some of the other educational innovators in this section, his work was much admired at the time and visitors came from other parts of the UK and Europe.

FRIEDRICH FROEBEL (1782–1852)

Froebel worked in Germany within the first half of the nineteenth century and was the founder of the kindergärten idea. He was impressed with Pestalozzi's work at the Yverdon Institute and sought ways to improve on the organisation to support the ideas.

With like-minded colleagues, Froebel opened a school in Keihau, in an area known then as Thuringia and later an infant school in Blankenburg, Prussia. This school for younger children was called a **Kindergärten** (literally the children's garden) and this term has been widely used since for establishments for children of four to six years of age. One of Froebel's most enthusiastic supporters, the Baroness of Marenholtz-Bulow, was mainly responsible for introducing his ideas to educators in England, France and The Netherlands.

Froebel's ideas may not seem extraordinary now, but they were at the time. He believed that teachers should encourage children's self-expression through individual and group play and through freely chosen activity. This approach contrasted sharply with educational practice in many European countries of that time that favoured repetitive drills and teacher-led routines. Froebel's ideas became the most significant throughout Europe, with the early educational methods of many countries strongly influenced by his approach.

JOÃO DE DEUS (1830–1896)

João de Deus was a lyric poet who exerted a significant influence on Portuguese literature at the end of the nineteenth century. At a time of his life when poetry made him only a limited living, de Deus became fascinated with developing a new method to teach children how to read and his method was officially adopted in Portugal in 1888 and he was appointed to manage its introduction. Some of Portugal's provision still follows de Deus' ideas.

MARIA MONTESSORI (1870–1952)

Montessori was based in Rome (Italy) and, like Ovide Decroly, first worked with disabled children before extending her approach to young children as a whole.

During the first decade of the twentieth century Montessori developed her educational methods from the belief that children need to escape the domination of parents and teachers. Adults should be more humble and less superior in their dealings with young children. She opened the first Casa dei Bambini (Children's House) in 1907.

Montessori developed an environment for children with methods and materials that were aimed to train the senses. Her aim was that children's spontaneous interest was enlisted appropriately at their varied stages of development. Children were enabled to master the basic skills of life through self education and exploration. The materials were designed to encourage individual rather than cooperative effort and group activity was encouraged through shared domestic responsibilities. Montessori travelled widely through Europe, India and the United States, finally settling in The Netherlands.

OVIDE DECROLY (1871–1932)

Decroly was based in Brussels (Belgium) and during the early part of the twentieth century he developed a programme of early education based on centres of interest and educational games for children. A key feature is the workshop-classroom in which children can freely chose their activities. A carefully organised curriculum was based on an analysis of individual children's needs in four areas of food, shelter, protection and work.

Current issues across the European Union

Children as citizens

A number of EU countries have or are in the process of rethinking provision for young children within a shift to development of family policies that place children in a more central position, rather than as an invisible group behind the adults.

A greater awareness of the need to address children's concerns has been partly economic. Many EU countries have experienced a declining fertility rate over the second half of the twentieth century (see page 4), so that quality of provision has seemed more important for the shrinking future labour force. Current labour shortages have also brought childcare onto the political agenda. Even the most blinkered politicians and planners realise that encouraging women who are mothers of young children back into the labour force is impossible without some attention to childcare provision.

High levels of poverty affecting children in some regions of EU countries have also raised the profile of quality provision for young children. The UK does not have a good record on child poverty. Poor households are defined as those with an equivalent income that falls below 50% of the average household income for that country. In 1994 the Statistical Office of the European Communities (EUROSTAT) estimated that over 20% of the children in EU countries (twelve EU members at that time) were living in poverty. However, the proportions varied, with the UK highest with 32% of children living in poverty and Denmark the lowest at 3%.

EU countries like Denmark and Sweden, and also Norway (non-EU) have made a specific political commitment to children as the youngest citizens, to whom the broader society has obligations. This perspective is an alternative to seeing children just as the responsibility of their own families. The commitment is reflected in efforts to integrate the different kinds of services for children and young people and to seek more effective involvement of parents and children in decision making. These countries have many differences but share a vision that children are part of society.

Separation of day care and early childhood education

Across Europe, provision for young children and their families has tended to develop in response to social need and separate systems of 'care' and 'education' are common. Early years practitioners in some countries have made persistent efforts to achieve some integration of the two systems, but in many cases separation is still a common feature of daily practice.

DAY CARE AS WELFARE

The orientation for the under threes is more usually that of caring for children in the context that their families cannot provide this care. The attitudes towards working mothers vary, but are sometimes still hostile. Individual day care settings may be very positive but the broader social context is often that they exist to deal with the social deficit of families whose mothers cannot or will not care for the younger children.

The different perspectives are also reflected in the distinctive patterns of training. Practitioners in the more care oriented settings follow different qualifications and training content than their colleagues in the educational settings. Working with under threes has traditionally required a more paramedical or social care orientation and working with the over threes a more educational orientation.

Some centres have worked actively to combine and integrate the two traditions, for instance the combined centres and the new early excellence centres in the UK. However, such innovatory developments have tended to be the exception and different systems of qualifications and job conditions still make such centres a bureaucratic headache for committed managers.

PROVISION FOR CHILDREN UNDER THREE YEARS

In most EU countries the level of provision for under threes is low, both in absolute numbers and in contrast to facilities for the over threes. Early education is usually envisaged as a provision for over threes and so any facilities for younger children fall within day care. Official responsibility then usually, although not always, falls within the national and local ministries or departments for social welfare.

The general level of provision for under threes is low in EU countries, because with few exceptions facilities for the youngest children are seen as linked with maternal employment or needy families who are unable to care effectively for their children. The increased levels of maternal employment

Children need space to play

in many EU countries have brought this issue to the forefront. However, an increased need for provision for under threes has not necessarily led to increased public provision or a broad change in the negative attitudes often expressed about facilities for the youngest children. This is in contrast to the more positive views usually held about early childhood education.

Family obligations and employment

WHY THE FOCUS ON MATERNAL EMPLOYMENT?

Care for children outside the family has developed historically in response to increased maternal employment. The cultural tradition of all European countries has been that mothers are seen as the primary carers of children. So, increases in the employment of women who are additionally mothers has raised the practical issue of who will care for the children while their mothers are at work. If care is not possible within the family, then other forms of non-family care are sought.

Increased female employment as a whole can impact on childcare, for instance when societies have depended on care by female relatives, frequently grandmothers. Late entry into the labour market or uninterrupted employment of the older female generation removes what was a traditional option of childcare within the family for the younger generation.

The level of employment of women who are mothers varies considerably across EU countries, although some are in the process of social change on this issue. Table 2.1 shows the levels of employment of parents with a child under fifteen years in 1993, in the twelve EU countries at the time.

The differences behind the averages in Table 2.1 vary for mothers' employment from 34% in Ireland and Spain to 70% in Portugal and 76% in Denmark. In Germany there was a noticeable difference between the old West Germany, with 50% and East with 72%. The proportion of mothers in the workforce with part-time jobs was also variable across the EU in 1993. Part-time work was especially high in The Netherlands, with 88% of employed mothers of under fifteens with part-time jobs. The UK had a figure of 64% and Germany of 60%. This situation contrasted with southern EU countries of Italy, Greece, Portugal and Spain where less than 20% of working mothers had part-time jobs.

Fathers' employment is much less varied across the EU countries. In 1993 90% of fathers with children under fifteen were employed and most of those classified as unemployed were seeking a job. In contrast, most of the mothers classified as unemployed were not seeking work, although surveys in some countries, for instance the UK, often indicate an interest to find work if childcare were to become a more realistic possibility. So the difference between the employment levels of mothers and fathers tends to reflect the social assumption in most EU countries that it is maternal employment that will depend on childcare. Fathers' employment can of

Table 2.1: Employment and unemployment: mothers and fathers with a child under 15: 1993

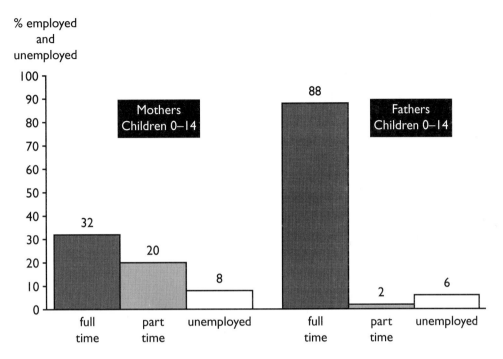

Source: Ria Meijvogel and Pat Petrie (1996) *School-age childcare in the European Union* (European Commission Network on Childcare)

course impact on family life especially when they work long hours. In 1993 for instance, UK fathers worked an average of 47 hours per week, 6 hours more than their contemporaries in The Netherlands, Belgium or Denmark.

AN ALTERNATIVE SOCIAL PERSPECTIVE

However, the firm links made between the need for day care and maternal employment rest on assumptions and values about how society works and the place of women and the family within it. An alternative perspective is to see non-parental day care as the result of both parents working or being absorbed in some other time-consuming activity like studying. The level of need for care outside the family is also determined by how employment is structured within a society.

In many EU countries, the UK included, most employment is organised on the assumption that workers do not have family responsibilities. Then, if workers obviously do have some obligations, the consequences are designated solely as a family issue and nothing to do with the employers.

Similar problems arise over care within the family of sick or elderly adult members; family responsibilities that can fail to fit with employment do not begin and end with care of young children.

An alternative scenario, more integral to the assumptions of some EU countries, such as Sweden and Denmark, is that a society needs a current labour force and also definitely needs at least a proportion of its population to produce and care for the next generation. Every society needs some of its population to make the choice to have children; it should not be seen as an activity characterised by personal indulgence. An alternative ethical stance is therefore that society should support childhood in general, families in particular and working parents without a sense of begrudging the help.

RECONCILIATION OF EMPLOYMENT WITH FAMILY RESPONSIBILITIES

Since the 1980s the EU has developed a significant body of policy about families and work obligations.

The European Commission Network on Childcare (whose publications are still a major source for material on countries in the EU) was funded from 1986 to 1996 by the Equal Opportunities Unit of the European Commission. The increased focus on placing childcare in a full social context led to the Network's full name to change in 1991 to become the European Commission Network on Childcare and other Measures to reconcile Employment and Family Responsibilities. The concept of reconciliation of employment and family life covers:

▶ Both men and women: that these issues are not seen just as problems for women to solve, with the view that they have chosen to be employed.
▶ The whole life span, not only families in the stage of raising young children. Care of sick family members or older relatives (sometimes called elder care) is also an issue.
▶ The re-allocation of family responsibilities within the home between men and women. If society wants more women in the labour force, then social attitudes have to change from believing that domestic responsibilities (sometimes called the 'social work load') can remain mainly female.
▶ The development of appropriate services and the responsiveness of the work environment and job conditions to family obligations.

The 1996 EU Directive on Parental and Family Leave required all member countries to develop a national system of employment contracts that ensure the right to a minimum of three months of parental leave on the birth or adoption of a child. There must also be provision for time off work for pressing family reasons such as sickness. However, individual countries are left to determine the details such as whether such leave is paid or not.

Two main types of leave are relevant to families:

▶ **Maternity leave** is the amount of time women are allowed to take off from their jobs before and after the birth of a child and still return to the same employment afterwards. Countries vary over how much time is allowed, in what way the allocation of time may be determined to the periods before and after birth and whether fathers are allowed to take any of the allocation. Payment levels also vary: flat rate, earnings related, unpaid.

▶ **Parental leave** is a term referring to other kinds of leave that are allowable to either parent from their work. This allowance, which may be paid or unpaid, is made to enable families to look after a child, care for a sick child or make arrangements for a child's welfare. Sometimes a broader based family leave may cover family care obligations or emergencies that are not necessarily about dependent children.

The transition into statutory schooling

There is no common age of entry to statutory schooling across the EU.

▶ In about half of the EU countries, compulsory schooling starts at six years.

▶ Ireland and Northern Ireland (part of the UK) start children at four years old. Children in Luxembourg also start at four years but non-attendance is not a legal requirement until six years.

▶ The UK (England, Scotland and Wales) and The Netherlands officially start children in school at five years. However, in both countries a considerable number of four year olds are already in primary school.

▶ Sweden, Denmark and Finland have the latest age of entry to compulsory education, starting their children at seven years, although Swedish schools now have to accept children at six years of age if their parents wish.

So, the statutory school starting age is often an inaccurate guide to what is actually happening with children. As a general pattern, where countries have a younger compulsory school age the services prior to that age tend to be less highly developed or regulated, and more within the private sector than services in those countries where, relatively speaking, there is a delayed entry to school.

The movement of children from pre-school facilities or home into the statutory school years is often seen as a transition that needs to be eased. An awareness of anomalies, and a concern about early educational opportunity, has led several EU countries to develop systems that will achieve some level of consistency or integration for the last years of pre-school and early primary years.

▶ Luxembourg's introduction of compulsory pre-schooling in 1992 aimed to improve the educational opportunities specifically for children of the minority ethnic groups, comprising 30% of the country's population.

▶ France and Belgium introduced the conceptual framework of cycles of learning, one of which bridges the ages at which children are at an école maternelle and the early years of primary school.

▶ At the time of writing (1999) there is a discussion ongoing in England and Wales within the UK about making nursery education for three to five year olds a Foundation Stage that runs into statutory schooling. Early years practitioners and professionals are cautious about the proposals since the change seems likely to involve a more formal, adult-led curriculum than has been regarded so far as good practice.

▶ Finland developed the framework of learning modules for five and six year olds that are used both within day care centres and schools.

▶ The Netherlands integrated pre-school education into the compulsory school system in 1985 and the training of the kindergarten teachers was also merged with that of the primary school teachers.

Services for school age children

Childcare is often discussed as if all problems disappear once children start compulsory schooling. However, the hours of most jobs, and certainly the full-time employment opportunities, are longer than the normal school day and terms in all EU countries. In many EU countries very limited attention has been given to the provision for school age children, although increased concern has been expressed throughout the 1990s.

Out-of-school provision that exists is often loosely regulated in the different EU countries and sometimes scarcely regulated at all. The services are varied and under the responsibility of different departments, so that even getting reliable statistics can be complicated. In the absence of provision, voluntary organisations have sometimes filled the gap. The different types of provision include:

▶ Separate centres for school age children that are regulated and may employ specially trained workers. Some facilities are run on school premises but others have their own building. Some facilities only run during term time whereas others cover school holidays.

▶ Ad hoc arrangements designed to 'wrap around' the school day to provide complete cover. Supervision might be offered within the school, some children move to and fro from an age integrated centre and some of the gaps are covered by family day carers.

▶ Open access (or drop-in) services that include adventure playgrounds, youth and leisure facilities. Staff may be qualified workers or volunteers. This provision does not offer out-of-school care as such, because children have the choice to come and go.

▶ A range of play schemes that cover the school holidays or part of the time. Workers on such schemes tend to have a varied background, often unqualified and with limited pre-scheme training.

THE PLAYWORK TRADITION

Some of the staff in out-of-school provision, both in care and open access facilities, have experience and perhaps also training within the tradition known as **playwork**.

Compared with day care or early childhood education, playwork is a young tradition, starting in the middle of the twentieth century. Open space playgrounds started through the vision of the Danish architect C. Th. Sorenson. His first 'junk playground' opened in Copenhagen in 1943 with the aim of giving children the freedom for exploration and choice in their own space and with a rich array of junk materials. The junk playground idea spread in Denmark and neighbouring European countries. Lady Allen of Hurtwood brought the idea to England in the late 1940s.

There was a steady growth of this facility and they became known as adventure playgrounds, with some fixed structures as well as a wide choice of building materials. The free choice playground concept, with its open access, does not merge comfortably with out-of-school care in which children become the responsibility of the adults for given hours of the day. There are some tensions, in the UK and some other EU countries, between the free choice playwork tradition and what has come to be called **playcare**. The playcare tradition does, however, have a long historical tradition at least in the UK, since supervised play centres started in the 1860s with the Settlement Movement.

The early years workforce

The vast majority of people working with young children either in day care or early education are women. The pattern of an overwhelmingly female workforce is common to most EU countries, although less marked in the Scandinavian countries. The early years workforce is at least 90–95% female in most EU countries and in day care facilities can be close to 100%. The blend of care and education towards an early years pedagogy in Scandinavia seems to have bring more mixed staff teams.

Generally, the older the age group of children, the more likely it is to find some males in the staff team, although even primary school teams are overwhelmingly female. The out-of-school provision, with its links to sport and leisure activities, is more likely to have some male workers.

Efforts to bring more men into the profession have faltered on the conviction in many countries that care, and early education, of young children is women's work. Poor pay and career prospects have further limited the entry of men. Like any profession dominated by one gender, men in early years have to face the minor and more major adjustments of work environments in which most people are the opposite gender. There is also the concern, more marked in some EU countries than others, that bringing men into the early years workforce will inevitably expose children to higher risks of abuse (see also page 19).

TRAINING AND QUALIFICATIONS

In many EU countries there has been some level of review and sometimes major changes in the pattern of staff who work with young children, the required qualifications and the regulated content of the courses that train students towards the appropriate qualifications. There has been a general trend to upgrade training courses: raising formal entry requirements, the length of the course, more demanding content and often integration into higher levels of the educational system, sometimes towards degree level. Consequently the majority of the staff in publicly funded provision are now trained to a more demanding level than in previous decades.

Some countries have also shared a concern to address the care-education split in terms of integrating a more educational approach into the more care or paramedical qualifications. The historical pattern in many EU countries has been that people who work with the younger age range, usually the under threes, tend to have lower formal educational qualifications and the courses have had a more social care or paramedical orientation. The concern of some practitioners, certainly in the UK, is that the vital care aspect is not pushed to one side but is rather blended with a learning orientation.

Rural issues

All EU countries have some rural areas but some have larger proportions of the total population in regions classified as rural. Rural areas share similar practical issues.

PROBLEMS FOR EARLY YEARS SERVICES

Some rural areas may look very attractive but can hide major practical problems for children and their families:

▶ Many rural areas have a sparse and scattered population. The low numbers of children in a single area can mean that funding centres for each village or small town is impractical.

▶ As a result, children often have to be transported to early years provision and primary school, either by publicly funded transport or being driven by their parents. Alternatively, early years services have to be mobile and come to the families.

▶ However, some rural areas have been repopulated by families who have chosen to move out of the city and child populations may not be so low. Such areas are often called peri-urban and may have working parents who commute long distances to their jobs. The areas can be lacking vital childcare facilities for such families.

▶ Some rural areas, such as mountainous areas or networks of islands, can be inaccessible, especially in times of bad weather.

A DIFFERENT RURAL APPROACH

Rural areas often need a different approach to early years provision and blithe urban assumptions can falter quickly. The national childcare policies of many EU countries are usually developed by politicians and practitioners who live and work in cities and towns. The Sure Start initiative in the UK from 1999 has had to recognise that bids for funding from rural areas are not developed around a single building and the concept of 'pram pushing' local distance that made sense in urban areas. Some of the rural bids have been worked around establishing or promoting a network of services, where 'pram pushing' distance can be a half-day hike.

TOURISM

Some rural areas are highly dependent on a seasonal tourism economy. Of course not all rural areas of the EU attract tourists, but in some of the southern EU countries in particular, such as Greece, most of the family income can depend on an intense few months in the summer. Such areas may have limited childcare provision and this can be much the same period when the primary schools are shut. There are no reliable statistics but it seems likely that families manage with informal systems including older siblings. Tourism is not only an issue in southern Europe. For instance, the publicity over the eclipse in Cornwall during the summer of 1999 highlighted just how crucial the seasonal tourist economy is to this part of England.

A SHARED PERSPECTIVE ON SIMILAR PROBLEMS

The HERA project that started in Suffolk, England in 1995 aimed to provide nationally recognised training to women at home caring for children. The project was funded for three years through the European Social Fund that was aimed at new employment opportunities for women.

Suffolk is a very rural county and project members made cross-national contacts with projects in Denmark, Spain and Greece that were also facing the special issues that arise in training and early years provision in rural, rather than urban, areas. The report of the HERA project highlights important lessons in cross-national contacts, including the need to anticipate different expectations from the different national teams and that good communications need to be established and maintained.

Making sense of cross-national statistics

Throughout Chapters 3 to 17 on the individual European countries you will find statistics on levels of provision, when they are available to quote. You will not find many direct comparisons between different countries because such an attempt has to be loaded with so many 'ifs' and 'buts' that the exercise becomes pointless.

Table 2.2 gives a comparison between countries of the European Union in their publicly funded services for children from birth to six years between 1991–4. These statistics were compiled by the European Commission Network on Childcare, who had the advantage of representatives in each country. (Luxembourg was not included because the data were very limited.) The Network discussion of their statistics offer an insight into the practical difficulties in making genuine sense of such figures.

Table 2.2: Levels of publicly funded services for young children: 1991–94

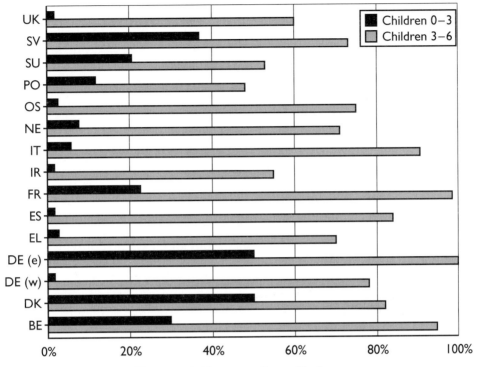

Places or children attending as % of age group

Key to countries:
UK: United Kingdom
SV: Sweden
SU: Finland
PO: Portugal
OS: Austria
NE: Netherlands
IT: Italy
IR: Ireland
FR: France
ES: Spain
EL: Greece
DE (e): East Germany
DE (w): West Germany
DK: Denmark
BE: Belgium

Source: European Commission Network on Childcare (1996) *A review of services for young children in the European Union 1990–1995*

Different national and regional systems

Making direct comparisons between different European countries is complicated because there is no single system for collecting information about provision for children across Europe. Additionally, within individual countries the responsibility for provision usually rests with more than one central or local government department.

There are confusions within as well as between countries. Countries, seen as a single entity by outsiders, can have wide internal differences between regions or communities who have some control over the development of local services. Statistics may be collected, and presented in a rather different way, by the educational departments and by social welfare and health within a single country.

It can be difficult to reach any firm conclusions about what is provided for families, the extent to which it is used and whether the provision meets what families would find most useful. In many EU countries the available statistics have gaps in information. Data are most often available on publicly provided services. Yet, there may be few, if any, reliable figures on privately funded or informal provision, that can be the main source for some families' needs.

Provision for the under threes

The data in Table 2.2 show striking differences between countries in their provision for the under threes. Countries such as Denmark and Sweden offer considerably greater provision for this age range than, for instance, the UK, Ireland or Spain. The contrast in provision between what was West and East Germany highlights the very different systems which were brought together in a new, unified Germany (see also page 98).

The countries where there is very low provision for under threes may have extensive informal arrangements which are used by parents, but official figures do not give information on this possibility. In the UK, for instance, surveys of families suggest that care by close relatives is a common way of dealing with the demands of paid work and childcare.

Low levels of provision for care of young children may matter less when parents have the right to take parental leave from their jobs. Parental leave is a term describing the right of parents to take time off work (paid or unpaid) around the birth or adoption and early years of their child.

Employment rates vary between European countries and so do policies on parental leave. More extensive parental leave has an impact on the kind of services that are appropriate and for what age range of children. Denmark, for instance, has sufficient publicly funded provision for about 50% of children from birth to three years. However, this country has a generous policy on parental leave, in comparison with many other EU countries, and there is lower demand for care of babies. Consequently, the available services are probably used more for the one to three year olds and as a result offer provision to a higher than 50% proportion of this group.

If countries have generous parental leave, there may be less demand for childcare provision for the very young. However, there may be a greater interest in services suitable for parents caring for their children, such as drop-in centres and play schemes where parents stay with their children. Carers within an informal network and carers paid by a family, such as childminders and nannies, may be potential users of the different kinds of provision other than full-time childcare centres.

Provision for children from three to six years

The Network used the common age bands of birth to three years and three to six years to make comparisons possible but the report notes that different countries operate varying ages of entry to statutory school (see page 35). So, the provision for the three to six year olds includes both statutory school attendance and early entry of younger children to primary school in some of the countries in Table 2.2. The kinds of pre-school provision included in the figures can vary considerably in terms of what children and their families are offered.

For instance, the most common forms of provision in Denmark for three and four year olds, such as the børnehaver, are open all the year round and for about 50 hours per week. On the other hand, the most common forms of provision for three and four year olds in the UK are pre-schools (known previously as playgroups and some groups still prefer that title) and nursery classes. The nursery classes follow school terms and holidays, and so do many pre-schools and playgroups. Many offer places to children on a sessional basis, so that a total week of attendance may be no more than 13 or 14 hours.

Different kinds of provision undoubtedly may suit different families and their needs. However, the greater extent of the Danish provision offers families a possible blend of childcare and education. Pre-schools, playgroups

and nursery classes in the United Kingdom cannot offer a provision that
meets any but the most restricted needs of working parents. Private nurseries
have grown to fill the childcare gap in the UK. The summary figures for the
two countries in Table 2.2 are a good example of how overall levels of
provision for an age range can only make sense with further details of what
kind of provision exists.

Quality and distribution of provision

There is no way of judging the quality of provision from the figures. The
provision included under the summary statistics may, or may not, be of an
acceptable standard, given a country's own methods of assessment or by
some more general approach to quality. For instance, many of the EU
countries stress that one issue in quality is the suitability and accessibility of
provision for disabled children and those with other special needs. However,
it is hard to assess the extent to which the provision meets this aspect to
quality.

Most EU countries also experience an uneven distribution of the provision
that is made available to families. This uneven spread is reflected in common
differences between availability in urban and rural areas. Denmark is one
exception to this more general pattern. Children in urban areas of Denmark
are more likely to be able to attend provision. However, the high levels of
provision nationally in Denmark create a situation where Danish rural areas
often have better levels of provision for children, including childcare, than
some of the urban areas of other EU countries.

Some rural areas in EU countries experience very limited provision. The
realistic opportunities for families in mountainous and other relatively
inaccessible areas bear no relationship to national percentages. For example,
in Macedonia (a region of northern Greece), difficult travelling conditions,
especially in winter, and widely distributed small communities lead to a
situation of limited provision for three to six year olds and sometimes no
provision at all for under threes.

Individual EU countries

The UK shares many issues and concerns with fellow countries in the
European Union. However, despite some elements of a shared European
past, the fifteen EU countries are very different in their social, political and
economic framework, let alone their early years and school services.

Each chapter from 3 to17 focusses on one country within the EU. They are listed alphabetically, which places the UK last in the line. You are welcome to read the chapters in the order you prefer but it is illuminating to read at least three or four descriptions of other countries and then to look at Chapter 17 on the UK. An increased awareness of other EU countries and systems throws a bright light on our own. As far as possible each chapter follows a similar pattern which covers:

- ▶ National background: geographical location, politics and government, economic and social issues including language, population and urban-rural divisions.
- ▶ Pre-school provision: day care centres, family day care, the situation on family obligations and employment, early childhood education, any other early years provision.
- ▶ Statutory education: primary schooling and out-of-school provision.

The main source of statistics remains the reviews and publications of the European Commission Network on Childcare (see page 195 for full references).

3

Austria

National background

Geographical location

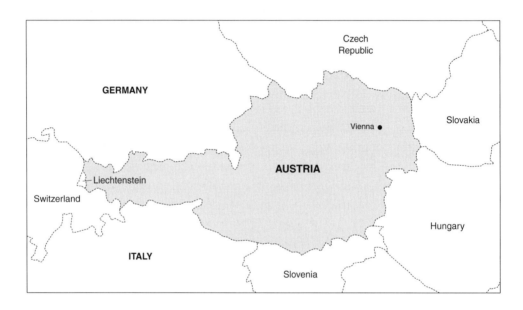

Austria is a scenic and mainly mountainous country. The Alpine region in the west occupies about two-thirds of the country's land and consequently Austria is among the most mountainous countries in Europe. Some mountains are higher than 3000 metres (10 000 feet). A further one-tenth of the land area is made up of the Bohemian Forest, a highland region reaching 1200 metres (4000 feet). The lowland region of Austria lies almost entirely in the eastern quarter of the country, although with elevations of between 150 to 400 metres (500–1300 feet), it is still hilly.

Austria's geographical position has contributed to its historical and continued importance in Europe. The country is located at the centre of traffic along the Danube river and lies between the Alpine passes to the north and south. Austria is completely land-locked: bordered by Germany, the Czech Republic and Slovakia in the north, by Hungary in the east, by Italy and Slovenia in the south and by Switzerland and Liechtenstein in the west.

Politics and government

Until the end of the First World War, Austria was at the political centre of the substantial Austro-Hungarian Empire, which included many areas now known as independent European countries. After 1918 Austria emerged as a separate nation, but then experienced a quarter of a century of social and political turbulence until the country was absorbed into the Nazi dictatorship established during the Second World War. In 1955 a permanent neutrality was created in Austria when the Allies' troops were withdrawn.

Austria is a republic with a democratic political system. The country has a federal system, somewhat similar to that of Germany, that brings together distinct regions under the central government. Austria has nine **Bundesländer** (provinces) that retain control of their internal affairs. However, the country forms a distinct political unity and operates as a single nation in foreign affairs. The national (federal) government can pass national legislation which the Bundesländer are obliged to follow. However, the regions operate with some level of independence in running local services within the defined legislative framework.

Social and economic framework

During the second half of the twentieth century, Austria has developed into a stable society, with a resurgence of the cultural life for which the country had been previously known. The economy has a moderate rate of growth and the standard of living is similar to that in other Western European countries. Manufacturing is an important part of the economy but tourism also plays a major part, with a summer and winter (skiing) season.

Austria joined the EU in 1995 at the same time as Finland and Sweden, this group having made the decision to leave EFTA (see page 10).

LANGUAGE

The main language of Austria is German. 98% of the population speak this language, which is a slightly different version from that spoken in Germany, although understandable to a German speaker.

Population

In 1998 the country had a population of 8.1 million, of whom 17% were under fifteen years of age. Austria has a zero annual population growth rate and an ageing population as a whole.

Urban-rural

There have been noticeable movements to the towns and cities and the growing urban population now accounts for two-thirds of the total.

Pre-school provision

Children start compulsory school at six years of age but the pre-school provision is a separate system. Children attend, or not, depending on the choice of their parents.

Under the terms of the Austrian constitution, the nine Bundesländer have been responsible, since 1962, for the development and implementation of legislation and policy of all childcare and education services, including family day care, which lies outside the compulsory school system.

The publicly funded services for children under school age are under the control of the Ministry of Family Affairs at national level and the Departments of Youth and Family Welfare in the Bundesländer. The regions control practical issues about pre-school provision, organisation and staffing, but training is determined at federal level. There are some common features in provision for the under and over threes, but Austria does not have an integrated system for all young children. There are no national required standards on staff-child ratios in non-school provision and standards are determined in the regions. In practice the adult-child ratio does not appear to vary much.

Day care centres

Kinderkrippen are full day nurseries run for children from birth to three years old, although the majority of children are two year olds, since this is the cut off for statutory parental leave. The Kinderkrippe are often associated with Kindergärtens for the over threes (see page 50) in that they are managed by the same local body and located on the same premises.

A Kinderkrippe is usually set up and managed by the regional family and youth authorities. The usual pattern is to have groups of 10 to 15 children in their own room, with four workers who organise their time in shifts to cover the whole day. The ratio is usually supposed to be held at 2:14, although it can vary between the regions. Two of the team of four are fully qualified **Kindergärtnerin** or **Kindergärtenpädagogin** (kindergärten teachers) and two are **Kindergärtenhelferin** (unqualified assistants). (Training is described on page 51.) The approach of the Kinderkrippe used to be mainly in terms of physical care, but the emphasis has shifted to a greater emphasis on social development and the needs of individual children.

The level of day care provision for under threes is very low and, along with Germany, Austria has one of the lowest levels in the EU. Facilities for the youngest children have been a low political priority and are seen as linked only to maternal employment rather than as an educational or social opportunity for children.

In 1995 there were places in Kinderkrippen for only about 3% of the under threes in Austria, but such places are distributed unevenly and about 75% of the national total of places are in Vienna (the capital). So in this city a higher proportion, about 10% of under threes, are able to attend.

Family day care

Private arrangements are made between some parents and providers of **Familientagespflege** (family day care) and this is a form of provision that has expanded during the 1990s.

Family day care is regulated by the regional authorities and providers need an official licence which states the maximum number of children and space requirements. Depending on housing conditions, a **Tagesmutter** (literally day mother) might be permitted to take up to seven children in total including her own. The arrangement is seen as one made by individual families and providers. The Tagesmutter can take children up to ten to twelve years, but family day care mainly meets the need for care of under threes. Family day care is an expanding part of provision and there are current discussions about ways that it could best work. The regional authorities often promote family day care as the most appropriate service for very young children of working parents. There are no reliable national statistics but the European Commission Network on Childcare (ECNC) estimated that in 1995 there were about 3000 family day carers taking responsibility for more than 6000 children.

Some training is available for family day carers and this is usually run by private organisations. Requirements on the scheme of training vary between the regions, depending on the local professional organisation for the family day carers.

Family obligations and employment

In 1993 64% of Austrian mothers with 0 to 15 year olds were in employment, about 62% of them on a full-time basis. This is the highest rate of employment of mothers in the EU countries besides Sweden, Denmark, Finland and Portugal. Parents, usually mothers, are encouraged to take extended parental leave with the incentive of payments. Austria provides a two-year period of leave but childcare arrangements for very young children then become problematic.

As described earlier, there is very limited day care through the Kindergrippen and the hours of the Kindergärten (nursery schools) may not fit even a part-time job. The need for quality day care for working parents has become an increasingly public issue in Austria. The greatest need seems to be for children of two and three years of age. Two years of Parental Leave seems to reduce the demand for day care until children reach two years of age and the Kindergärten are of some help when they reach four years of age, although some additional care source may be needed. Employees have a statutory right to one week of paid leave per year to look after a sick family member and a further week to care for a sick child under eleven years of age.

In 1994 more than 80% of children under two years of age had a parent on Parental Leave, while about 3% were attending a publicly funded childcare service. By two and three years, about 20% attended a publicly funded service rising to more than 80% for the four and five year olds.

Early childhood education

Kindergärtens are provided for three to six year olds and about in 1994 about 75% of the age range was attending this form of provision. This percentage includes a variation within the age range: close to 100% of five year olds attend, between 70–80% of four year olds and a lower rate for three year olds, varying between as low as 20% in some regions to a high of 60% in Vienna.

The aim of the Kindergärtens is to complement parents' input and to provide a well-rounded curriculum for children's development within their peer groups. The Kindergärten approach aims to prepare children for school in a way that will create equal chances for all children. Some of the Bundesländer have established regional legislation that encourages an educational focus in Kindergärten morning sessions followed by smaller afternoon groups that emphasise more emotional and recreational needs for children.

Groups can be 25 to 28 children in size and are the responsibility of a **Kindergärtnerin** or **Kindergärtenpädagogin** who is a qualified Kindergärten educator, usually supported by one unqualified assistant between two groups. The ratio can vary between the regions but is usually held at about 2:23. The Kindergärtnerin training lasts for five years when young people start at fifteen and for two years after Austria's equivalent to our A levels. With further specialised training it is possible to work with disabled children as a **Sonderkindergärtnerin**.

Slightly over half (53.5%) of the Kindergärtens offer a full day (similar to the Austrian school day), 22.6% a full day but with a mid-day break and 23% operate on a half day basis. The Kindergärten opening hours vary considerably between the different Bundesländer, with the highest proportion of full day Kindergärtens in Vienna (93%) and the lowest in Tyrol and Voralberg (5%). Fees also vary between the regions and are usually related to family income.

In theory, children can attend a Kindergärten from three years old but some of the regions give priority to four year olds, preferring that younger children attend family day care or other services. Some Kindergärtens have mixed age groups, which include school age children in the afternoon (after the end of the school day) and such groups are called **Familiengruppen**.

The number of Kindergärtens has been increasing steadily since the 1970s. The Kindergärtens are the responsibility of the individual Bundesländer, except that the national Ministry of Education and Cultural Affairs retains responsibility for the training and employment conditions of the kindergärten staff. About three-quarters of the Kindergärten are run by public authorities and about a quarter by private welfare organisations, most of which are Catholic organisations. There is no national curriculum for the Kindergärten.

Parent-led groups

The availability of more and appropriate childcare for working parents has become a prominent political issue in Austria and there has been an expansion during the 1990s of a range of parent-led new groups.

Groups are called **Selbstorganisierte Kindergruppe** (self-organised children's groups) or **Elterninitiativen** (parent-initiated or led). Such groups have been organised and started by parents in order to cover the different needs from birth to fifteen years, although most are for children from one to six years. Groups have been started for different reasons: the lack of appropriate local services, long waiting lists and the desire to implement a preferred educational approach.

Such groups have to follow relevant legislation set by the regional authorities, but some regions place few if any conditions on the parent-led groups. Fees are usually met partly through state subsidy, although the level of public funding varies between the regions and by parental contribution. The ECNC estimated in 1995 there were about 300 parent-led groups, catering to over 3000 children.

The opening hours vary according to the needs of the families who set up the group and may be as short as ten hours or as long as forty hours in a week. The organisation is usually that groups of 10 to 11 children are supervised by a worker. Staff may or may not be qualified, depending on the requirements of the Bundesländ. There is now a national organisation of the parent-run centres and they run short courses to qualify for work in these centres.

Support services

Some regions offer support services through **Eltern-Kind-Zentrum** (parent and child centres) which combine activities, parental support and services for young children. **Kinderspielgruppen** (literally child playgroups) offer groups for three and four year olds a few times a week in which parental support is an aim, although parents do not have to attend with their children.

Approaches vary across the EU towards partnerships with parents

Statutory education

Primary schooling

The schools are the responsibility of the federal Ministry of Education and the regional education departments.

In Austria children start school on the 1 September following their sixth birthday. Children are interviewed by the school head who makes a decision whether the child is ready for the demands of school, or can be admitted slightly younger than six years. There is only one entry to school each year and children who are not yet ready may continue in Kindergärten or attend a pre-primary year. Children have to attend school until fifteen years of age. Schooling is free.

The pre-primary year, known as **Vorschulstufe** or **Vorschulklassen** is intended for children who have reached the age of compulsory schooling but who are still not mature enough to attend full school. The Vorschulstufe is part of the official school system and aims to prepare children for school life. Parents can ask for their children, who are not yet six years old and who were not offered early admission, to attend Vorschulstufe on a voluntary basis. Again the aim is to prepare children for school.

The Austrian school day ends around lunchtime or soon afterwards and most schools do not provide lunch to children. The difference between the school holidays and the average annual leave for employed adults is 8.5 weeks. Consequently the difference between working days and the year and the school hours and terms leaves a significant childcare gap.

Out-of-school provision

There is some regulated out-of-school provision, but not sufficient to meet demand, although between 1988 and 1995 there was a 24% increase in the level of out-of-school provision.

The established centres are called **Kinderhorte**, or just **Horte**, and tend to include six to ten year olds. The hours usually cover after school, the school holidays and any designated school-free days. In Austria all school children, including the youngest, are given homework, which traditionally they have completed at home with the help of their mother, on the assumption that she would not be working. It is understood that out-of-school services should create an environment in which children can complete their homework, before they go on to choose play and leisure activities.

Groups of about 21 children are supervised by a **Horterzieherin**, who is a Kindergärtenpädagogin who has undertaken additional training to equip the individual for working with school age children. This worker is supported by a non-qualified assistant. Over half of the available provision is managed by the local authorities, the rest by private or non-profit-making organisations.

Publicly funded centres that exist offer provision only to about 6% of six to ten year olds and the Kinderhorte are unevenly distributed around the country. For instance, 60% of the national total of out-of-school places are in Vienna. Most of the out-of-school places are provided in centres that are separate from schools, although some schools offer a care and recreation service on site and are known as **Tagesheimschule**. The regions determine the standards for out-of-school provision and so requirements vary across Austria. The ratio tends to average at about 1:15.5 school age children.

There are some age-integrated centres offering a service for children from birth to fourteen years on a full-day, year-round basis. These centres are called **Kinderhauser** or **Tagesheimzentrum** and they are not a common form of provision. A small number of schools have developed a pattern of full day opening within the school year and are known as **Ganztagsschule** (all day schools).

4

Belgium

National background

Geographical location

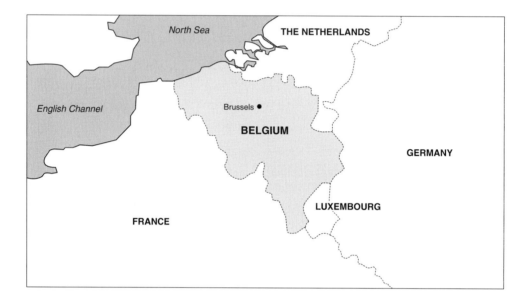

Belgium is located in the northern part of Europe and is generally a low-lying country. There is a broad coastal plain that rises gradually to the south-east but the highest point in Belgium is 694 metres (2277 feet).

The country has a coastline on the North Sea and the region of Flanders has areas of land (polders) that have been reclaimed from the sea in a similar system of dykes and drainage to The Netherlands close by. Belgium is bounded on the land side by France in the south, Luxembourg in the south-east, Germany in the east and The Netherlands in the north to north-east.

Politics and government

Belgium has a constitutional monarchy in which the monarch is the Chief of
State but has limited real power. The government is a democratic system
and became a federal state in 1970 largely because of the tensions between
the different language and cultural groups in the country.

Belgium has three distinct and official communities: Flemish, French and
German. The national government now shares power with the executive
and legislative bodies that represent the three communities. The
communities are further subdivided into provinces and then communes.

During the nineteenth and early twentieth centuries there was considerable
resentment within the Flemish community about the perceived dominance
of French speakers in the country's professional and administrative levels.
Political and economic changes in the 1970s to 1990s brought a greater
balance and regional autonomy but some level of controversy still remains
between the French and Flemish communities.

Social and economic framework

Belgium has some mining and heavy industry, although this part of the
national economy has been in decline. Engineering, manufacturing,
commerce and services remain important, with agriculture of lower
significance in Belgium's economy.

Belgium's social structure only makes sense with an understanding of the
different language communities.

▶ The Flemish community is located in the north of the country and
constitutes more than half of Belgium's population.
▶ In the South of Belgium the Walloon community comprises about
one-third of the country's population.
▶ The German speaking community in the East is the smallest of the
groups, with fewer than 1% of the population.

Belgium was one of the original group of six countries who formed what
became the EU in 1958.

LANGUAGE

Language is an important feature in Belgium's social and political life:

▶ The Flemish community speaks Netherlandic. English speakers tend to
call the Netherlandic spoken in Belgium 'Flemish' and that spoken in

The Netherlands as 'Dutch', but the language is very much the same. Netherlandic is also spoken in a small part of neighbouring France.

▶ The Walloon community speaks French, again very similar to that spoken in France.

▶ About one-tenth of the population is completely bilingual but most have at least some working knowledge of French and Netherlandic. Brussels (the capital) operates as a bilingual French-Netherlandic speaking area.

▶ The German speaking community in the East is the smallest of the official language communities.

▶ Foreign-born workers bring a range of other languages, mainly from countries around the Mediterranean, especially Italy, the Middle East and North Africa.

Population

In 1998 the total population was 10.2 million, of whom 18% were under fifteen years of age. The annual growth rate of the Belgian population is very low. The birth rate combined with immigration only just exceeds the result of emigration and the death rate. In 1993 the fertility rate nationally was 1.59.

Belgium's foreign-born population has a higher birth rate and some foreign workers return to their country of origin each year. This part of the workforce is concentrated in the Walloon mining and industrial regions and in the cities of Brussels and Antwerp.

Urban-rural

Throughout the twentieth century there has been significant movement from rural to urban areas so that Belgium is now one of the world's most urbanised nations. When Wallonia and Flanders became officially unilingual regions, the migration between the areas declined but there remain high levels of population movement within each region.

It is estimated that about a quarter of the population of Belgium lives in areas classified as rural and which cover about a half of the country's land. However, these rural areas are increasingly becoming peri-urban with residents commuting into jobs in towns and cities.

Pre-school provision

From 1989 each community became responsible for the childcare and educational services in that area. The childcare and education systems of each community are similar although not identical.

Each of the language communities in Belgium has a day care sector for children under three years of age and pre-primary schooling system for children from two and a half to six years of age. The two systems are distinct in ideology as well as politically and administratively. The services for under threes are part of the community welfare departments, whereas early years education for children from two and a half years is the responsibility of the local education departments. Publicly funded services may be run by the local authorities or private organisations.

Day care centres

In contrast to the long tradition of early years education for children over three years, provision for younger children is a much more recent development.

There are two main types of day care centre for under threes, all of which are open for 10 to 12 hours on a daily basis:

▶ Centres for children from birth to three years old, called **crèche**, **kribbe** or **kinderdagverblijf**, **Krippe** in the different language communities. These centres are open on a full-day, year-round basis.
▶ Centres for children from one and a half years to three years, called **prégardiennat** or **peutertuinen**. These centres are similar to the crèches as above but do not take very young children.
▶ The French-speaking community has a small number of full-day children's centres, mainly in rural areas, called **maison communale d'accueil de l'enfance**. These centres offer care from birth to six years, with varying hours. They tend to be privately run.

Approximately 30% of under threes attend some form of day care place but these figures include family day care. The European Commission Network on Childcare (ECNC) in their 1996 review explained the variety within this 30% national figure.

▶ In the French community in 1993 27% of under threes had a place, but more than half of these places were those of two and half year olds in pre-primary schooling (see page 62). The remainder were divided between day care settings and family day care.
▶ In the Flemish community more than half of the places for under threes were in pre-primary schooling and even more of the remainder within family day care than was the case for the French pattern.

▶ Places for under threes in the German community were all within family day care and covered 13% of the age group.

Each kind of day care centre is usually staffed by nursery workers who have a more medically oriented training. Larger centres are more likely to have medical nurses and social workers on the team. Centre managers are usually medical nurses and the larger nurseries are required to have this type of qualified manager. The nursery workers are called **puéricultrice** and are less highly qualified than workers of the same title in France, in that these workers tend to have a two year vocational training. This kind of worker is called a **kinderverzorgster** or **Kinderpfleger/in** in the other communities. The staff with a social work background are called **assistante sociale** or **maatschappelijk werk(st)er**. The nursing qualification required for managers of larger centres is that of **infirmière**, **verpleegkundige** or **Krankenschwester**.

A debate has developed within Belgium, especially within the French-speaking community, about the training of workers with under threes. There has also been some pressure towards bringing a stronger educational orientation into what is seen as too much of a custodial care system, but the thrust is still mainly paramedical.

Parents pay a fee for day care places and any regulations and forms of organisation for the settings are less centralised and standard than for the pre-primary settings. Ratios of adults to children in the French community crèches are about 2.5 adults:12 children. The ratios are reached by requirements that there is one puéricultrice for every seven children under three years and that the centre has one infirmière and half an assistante for every 48 children. The prégardiennat tends to have a ratio of 1 puéricultrice:9 children and an additional one infirmière and half an assistante for every 48 children. The maisons communales tend to have a ratio of about 2:9.

Provision of day care is limited in rural areas and private provision is sometimes very expensive. Family day care is more of a possibility but still relatively inaccessible in some areas of the country.

Family day care

Family day carers in Belgium are self employed or may be part of an organised scheme. The carers are known as **gardienne** (French) or **opvanggezin** (Flemish). If the carers are in an organised scheme the system is known as a **gardienne encadrée** or **dienst voor opvanggezin**. Self employed family day carers are known in full as **gardienne indépendante** or **particulier opvanggezin**. A family day carer can take up to three children in the French community and four in the Flemish. The family day carers groups have to be supervised by one infirmière or an assistante sociale for every twenty carers.

Previously family day carers were not required to undertake training but there have been changes during the 1990s. The French community requires carers to undertake continuous training to be part of a scheme and independent carers to have relevant experience or training in order to be approved by the local authority.

Family obligations and employment

Provision has been responsive in part to the steady increase in the employment of women with children. In 1993 62% of women with a child under fifteen years were employed, 62% of them on a full-time basis. Services in the French community have a longer tradition of addressing the childcare needs of employed parents as well as social protection of disadvantaged children. In the Flemish community it was not really until the 1980s that support for the childcare needs of working parents became more of an avowed political aim of day care.

In Belgium as a whole there is up to 27 months of combined maternity and parental leave (not necessarily paid nor offered by all employers) after the birth of each child. Employees are also allowed some leave for family reasons: up to four days paid leave in the public sector and ten days unpaid in the private.

Early childhood education

Belgium has a long tradition of publicly funded early childhood education centres, starting with centres at the end of the nineteenth century based on the educational ideas of Friedrich Froebel and later reflecting the approach of Maria Montessori and Ovide Decroly (see pages 27 and 28).

Pre-school education is voluntary but most children attend. Pre-school centres provide for about 95% of three to six year olds over the whole country. Some centres will admit children as young as two and a half years of age, although concern has been expressed about the suitability of putting children so young into the larger groups of the pre-school centres. These

facilities are available and free for all the communities and known as
kleuteronderwijs or **kleuterschool** (Flemish), **école maternelle** (French)
and **Vorschule** or **Kindergärten** (German).

Most facilities are attached to primary schools and only about 5% are
separate settings with their own administration. The centres tend to follow
school opening hours and terms. They are usually maintained by the local
authority, but may be run by private organisations. The centres fall within
the responsibility of the relevant community Ministry or Department of
Education. In each community there are three main pre-school provision
networks. These include the official Community schools, grant-aided
schools, also called voluntary or 'free' schools, and often run by a Catholic
organising body and official grant-aided schools.

Pre-school education is free and the grant-aided schools are not permitted to
charge a fee. Parents can only be asked to make a contribution to items such
as school lunch, transport or out-of-school supervision. Pre-school settings
tend to run morning and afternoon sessions, although some offer a slightly
extended day and lunchtime supervision. Since the pre-primary groups
require a minimum number of children to be viable, some rural areas do not
have this form of provision.

The pre-primary system is highly regulated and consistent across settings in
terms of staffing and organisation. Each community will only make grants to
schools that meet legal requirements about curriculum and the inspection
standards. The staff complete a three-year training within higher education
that is aimed at this age range. Within the different language communities
staff are called **instituteur/institutrice de maternelle (**or **pré-scolaire)**,
kleuterleidster or **Kindergärtner/in**. The ratio is one teacher for every
nineteen children.

The philosophy is overtly educational with the focus generally on teacher-
structured activities. Pre-school settings have flexibility to determine their
curriculum, although the French community has an official pre-school
programme. The avowed aims of pre-school education in Belgium tend to
include social skills and cognitive and emotional development, as well as
some preparation for school. The denominational 'free' schools include
religious objectives. In Flanders there has been some exploration towards
more experiential learning for the children and encouraging teachers to
observe individuals and view the day more from the children's perspective.
Partnership with parents is not an explicit goal.

Transition from pre-primary to primary

The French-speaking community in Belgium has introduced the concept of **cycles of learning**, rather like the French system (see page 91). One such cycle aims to bridge the transition between the pre-school centres and the primary schooling stage. There are also discussions ongoing about a possible integrated course of training for pre-primary and primary level teachers.

Nursery education remains a separate level but, with primary education, it does form what is called basic education, **basisonderwijs** in the Flemish community and **ensignement** in the French, to cover from ages two and a half years to twelve.

Statutory education

Primary schooling

Children start school officially at six years of age and the language of instruction is French, Netherlandic or German, depending on the region. The central government transferred responsibility for education to the communities from 1989. There is a dual system of state and 'free' schools, the latter being mainly Catholic schools. The free schools have a government subsidy to enable them to be consistent with the state schools and not charge fees.

Children in the pre-primary system need additional facilities if their parents work a usual day because centres can close for a mid-day break. Schools tend to close mid-afternoon, with Wednesday afternoon closed and may or may not offer supervision for the mid-day break. The difference between school holidays and the average leave for employed parents can be as much as 10 to 11 weeks.

Out-of-school provision

There are some wrap-around arrangements on school premises financed by the local social services, but details vary considerably and there are no reliable national statistics on the amount of out-of-school care. There appear to be more facilities in urban than in rural areas. School-based facilities often developed as a resource for children who found it hard to study in peace at home, but over time some families began to use the service as a form of childcare.

The shift into school work is an issue for all EU countries

In the French community out-of-school care is usually provided in a school-based centre, **garderie scholaire,** and may be managed by the local authority or, in the case of private subsidised schools, by the governing body. In the Flemish community more centres are independent of schools and managed by the local authority. The Flemish school-based out-of-hours service is called **bewaking** and the separate centre **initiatief voor buitenschoolse opvang**. In the Flemish community, school age children may also be offered care in the family day care system.

The staff may be qualified or not, paid or voluntary and the programme for children differs. Qualified staff may have the diploma that leads to becoming an **éducateur** or **opvoeder**.

Holiday playschemes where they exist are increasingly taking on the role of providing provision for the older children. These schemes are called **plaine de jeu orspeelpleinen**. Children's clubs have expanded with funding from the Community Departments of Employment and these centres tend to have more of a playwork philosophy in contrast to the sometimes more custodial orientation of provision on school premises. In the German speaking community a holiday project has been organised through the local family day care bureau.

However, provision is developing in an unplanned way in response to pressing need and there is generally less provision in rural areas. The gap in services for children of school age is a matter for debate, especially in the Flemish-speaking community where public policy and standards were debated in the 1990s. There are no required adult:child ratios for out-of-school provision.

5

Denmark

National background

Geographical location

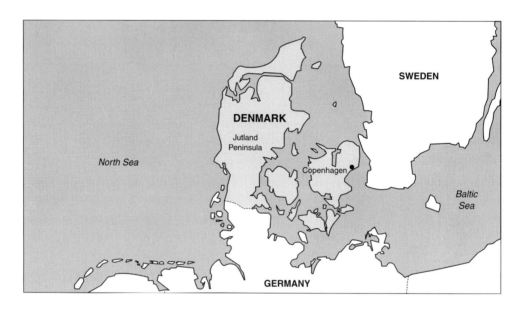

Denmark is located on the substantial Jutland peninsula stretching from the north aspect of mainland Europe with the North Sea on the west and the Baltic Sea and southern part of Sweden across the water in the east. Denmark's only land boundary is a 42 mile long boundary with Germany in the south.

Denmark, one of the smallest countries in the EU, also includes a total of four hundred large and smaller islands. The capital city of Copenhagen is situated on the largest island, Zealand. The Faroe Islands (located north-east from the tip of Scotland) also form part of Denmark. Greenland used to be part of the Danish political and administrative structure, but is now an independent country.

Politics and government

Denmark has a constitutional monarchy in that the monarch signs Acts passed by the Danish parliament. The country has a decentralised administrative structure such that control lies with the municipalities.

The aim of decentralisation was to enable a participatory process in each area that could address individual and regional needs. The municipalities have to follow any national legislation but are otherwise independent, politically governed and integral units within the country. Central government remains responsible for the overall control of development in key areas of the social sector. It establishes the broad legislative and financial framework for social policy but does not control and rule the outcome in detail. Denmark is divided into 14 counties and 275 municipalities or local authorities. The Faroe Islands have their own government, although foreign policy and defence remain under Danish control.

Denmark retains close links with other countries in Scandinavia. The group allow free movement without passports and operate an open labour market that includes reciprocal social welfare benefits and the right to vote in local elections in neighbouring countries.

Social and economic framework

Denmark's economy is mainly based on service industries, trade and manufacturing, with less importance for agriculture. Denmark supports a high standard of living and the Danish tradition is of a strong welfare and health system, the benefits of which are viewed as the rights of citizens who pay for the services through their taxes.

Denmark joined the EU in 1973, the first of the Nordic countries to do so. They joined with the UK, who was then Denmark's most important trading partner.

LANGUAGE

The main language is Danish, which is closely related to Norwegian, especially in its written form. Many educated or urban Danes have learned to speak a second language, often German or English.

Other languages have entered Denmark with the foreign-born 'guest workers' who have come mainly from Turkey, the former Yugoslavia, Iran and Pakistan.

POPULATION

For many years the total population of Denmark has only just been maintained. The fertility rate in 1992 was 1.76. In 1998 the Danish population totalled 5.3 million of whom 18% were under 15 years of age. This same proportion was 26% in 1950 and indicates the relative ageing of the population that Denmark shares with many other EU countries.

URBAN-RURAL

After some migration from urban to rural areas in the 1980s, the distribution of the population is fairly stable. In 1990 between 15 to 20% of the Danish population lived in rural areas in contrast to half the population in the 1920s. Some areas of Denmark are relatively remote and rural, especially some of the islands.

Pre-school provision

The Danish system has a long history which started in the nineteenth century with kindergartens based on Froebel's ideas, as well as settings with a more custodial philosophy. Towards the end of the nineteenth century an attempt was made to combine the different types into full-day public kindergartens. However, the greatest expansion of provision took place in the last three decades of the twentieth century.

An integrated system

The national Ministry for Social Affairs sets out a basic framework and conditions for early years provision. However, each municipality is then responsible for the provision, administration and inspection of all publicly funded provision. National guidelines and regulation exist for the provision but individual centres can still operate with a great deal of autonomy within this broad framework, including management of their budget. Locally, the early years provision also comes under the responsibility of social welfare departments. However, Denmark is striking in that the system it has developed over the last three decades of the twentieth century has none of the overtones of children in social need that bedevil services under social welfare departments in many other EU countries.

In 1987 the move was made to integrate policies for children, young people and families into all the areas of national political decision making. To this end Denmark has an Inter-Ministerial Committee on Children which brings together the representatives from fifteen relevant national ministries and is chaired by the Ministry of Social Affairs.

THE BLENDING OF CARE AND EDUCATION

Denmark is unusual in the European context for having a clear policy of bridging the care-education split and establishing a coordinated public system of **early years pedagogy**, also called **educare** by English commentators. The approach focusses on learning with scope for children's choices and an absence of adult-determined outcomes and tasks. Many settings organise children into mixed age grouping to offer the benefits of relationships across the years of childhood.

The educational philosophy still draws on Froebel and Montessori but with a specific Scandinavian flavour. A primary goal is to enable children to understand how they can be an active part of what happens in their immediate surroundings. Child-initiated play is therefore central. The goal of supporting the independent development of each child is pursued by the requirement to listen to children and to make them active participants in the planning of activities in any centre. In principle the early years settings can determine their own programme of activities. However, in practice the local municipality and parents' committees will set guidelines for the curriculum. There are no standardised national regulations or inspection systems and great reliance is placed on the professionalism of the early years workforce and the influence of parents.

All early years provision is optional, although the majority of Danish families take advantage of the opportunities for their children. The Danish approach is to value families and view them as central to children's continued well being, and to regard good quality early years provision as a social right to be provided by the state.

The range of settings

The following settings are usually open on a full-day, all-year-round basis. They all therefore offer full day care to children and are regulated to a limited extent by the national Ministry of Social Affairs, but administrative responsibility is usually delegated to the municipalities. Many of these centres are publicly run by the local authorities but a substantial minority (about 40%) are run by private, non-profit-making organisations.

Vuggestuer cater to children from birth (often six months) to two or three years (11.6% of age group). The children are usually in mixed age groups and have a key worker. Some staff are qualified **paedagoger** and have the support of assistants. These settings are more usual in large towns.

Børnehaver cater for three to five or six year olds (49.2% of the age group). Some staff are qualified paedagoger and some have no formal qualifications, although most have usually attended a local authority course. These settings are more evenly distributed between urban and rural areas.

Aldersintegrerede institutioner are age-integrated centres that cover from birth (usually six months) to six years and sometimes older, to twelve or fourteen years of age. About 2% of children from birth to two years and 25.4% of three to five year olds attend such settings. These centres were first developed in the 1970s and about 20% of children up to the age of nine years attend an age-integrated centre. The precise age range varies and in the 1990s there was a move to combine vuggestuer and børnehaver to form centres that covered from birth to six years.

The adult–child ratios are determined locally, since there are no national requirements. The European Commission Network on Childcare (ECNC) described the most usual ratios as 1:3 for children under three years of age, 1:6 for three to six year olds and 1:8 for six to ten year olds.

In 1995 the ECNC estimated that about 48% of Danish under threes attended some form of publicly funded provision, over half of which were in family day care (58%) and the rest divided equally between vuggestuer and aldersintegrerede institutioner. At the same time about 82% of three to six-year-olds attended publicly funded services. Of this group, 67% attended børnehaver, 26% were in aldersintegrerede institutioner and a minority (7%) in family day care. Nearly all six year olds attend the pre-primary classes (see page 73) but about two-thirds of these children also attend another publicly funded care or recreation service since the børnehaveklasser are mornings only.

Although Denmark has a high level of provision, the requests for day care usually exceed the local supply of places. Municipalities operate waiting lists and are able to give priority to children of lone parents, those who have both parents working or who have special social, educational or medical needs.

DISABLED CHILDREN

The Danish system has an explicit aim that disabled children should join mainstream settings wherever possible, often with additional support as appropriate. Separate settings are also available or a specialist group attached to a centre.

RURAL AREAS

Since Denmark has a high level of early years provision, the possibilities in rural areas are considerably better than in many other EU countries. However, on a national basis, the rural areas have less choice and access to services than urban families.

A FOCUS ON THE OUTDOORS

Early years provision for Danish children places a strong positive emphasis on outdoor play and exploration. Children are encouraged and enabled to spend plenty of time outdoors in the gardens or playgrounds of a setting. However, the approach also values regular trips to explore the locality.

Some børnehaver have located almost entirely outdoors and are called **skovbørnehaver** (forest school or kindergarten). This form of provision uses the outdoors in a deliberate way as part of children's learning of practical and social skills and an independent approach to safety issues. The skovbørnehaver take the group of children and staff out to the countryside for the day. The group may have access to a building but mainly spend their time outdoors. Some børnehaver make the countryside experience available to groups of children in turn. The countryside has been part of early years experience for Danish children since the 1980s, but the skovbørnehaver grew during the 1990s to between 2–300 in total.

PARTNERSHIP WITH PARENTS

Close involvement of parents, including at decision-making level, is a central feature of Danish provision. Partnership with parents is an explicit part of provision and it is usual practice for centres to have an elected committee that includes parents.

Since 1993 every municipal setting has to have a parents' committee and this group has the ability to influence staff recruitment, the curriculum and parts of the budget. The centre director has administrative and educational responsibility and implements the decisions of the parents' committee.

Training

In 1992 the aim of an integrated system for children was supported by reorganisation of the different strands of training.

The Danish system now trains paedagoger to be qualified to work with all the age groups, including school age children in after-school provision, and with disabled children. The paedagoger are trained within higher education in institutions specialising in this form of training on a course that lasts for three and half years. The training cannot be started until eighteen years but most of the workers do not start until they are in their twenties.

The paedagoger have a career path and positive self image that is different from that of school teachers. This positive image may influence a more definite career choice by older workers than is often the case in particularly the day care settings of some other EU countries. In the different centres, trained staff are usually supported by unqualified assistants, who may have attended a local course.

In Denmark there is a national debate about the value of more men in early years services and this discussion is grounded in gender equality issues rather than the child protection concerns typical of the UK. In 1995 a campaign was launched to encourage more men to train as paedagoger and in 1995 the new college intake was about 20% male. Although still a minority, this percentage is still much higher than most other EU countries.

Good provision for children needs outdoor space

Pre-primary schooling

Børnehaverklasser cater to six year olds in the year before they start compulsory schooling and operate as pre-school classes attached to a primary school. Some five year olds may be allowed to attend if they are judged to be mature enough to cope with the group. These settings run in the mornings only and are the responsibility of the national Ministry of Education. They are free to parents.

Staff are often paedagoger who work in the pre-primary class in the mornings and in the after-school facilities in the afternoon. The aim is that these classes support the transition of children into compulsory schooling. Consequently the curriculum is expected to have some features in common with schools although children are not yet formally taught. The majority of six year olds (about 98%) attend the børnehaverklasser.

Private sector

There is also a substantial independent sector that has privately run settings that receive some municipal funding.

The **puljeininstitutioner** or **puljeordninger** (the pool scheme centres) mainly cater for children from three to ten years of age. A parents' committee manages the institution and makes decisions about use of the public grants and appointment of staff. Parent-instigated private settings of this nature quite often meet the needs in rural areas and tend to offer a full-day, all-year-round service.

Family day care

Kommunal dagpleje is the term for provision through family day care and is a matter of individual agreement between the day carer and the family. However, this kind of provision is publicly funded and the family day carers are recruited, employed and partly paid by the local social services (parents usually pay about 30% of the cost). Dagpleje falls within the responsibility of the Ministry of Social Affairs in each municipality and the local carers may be supervised by an advisory worker.

The development of family day care from the late 1960s was originally seen as a stop-gap measure until sufficient day care group places had been developed. However, family day care continues to play a part in the Danish system, mainly for younger children but also for older ones, especially in the rural areas of the country. During the 1990s the perspective became one more of offering a range of day care services to families, of which nurseries were one option.

Family day carers cover from birth to six years and sometimes care for older children. They are limited to five children per carer. This form of provision is more used for the younger children and in 1995 33.5% of six months to two year olds and 5.7% of three to five year olds were in family day care. The system of provision is the responsibility of the local social services of the municipalities.

Family day carers are not necessarily qualified, but they usually attend local courses and meetings with other family day carers. In some cases, two carers will work together as a team providing family day care, called **stordagpleje**.

Family obligations and employment

Day care has increased in response to levels of employment of parents. However the facility is viewed as valuable for children and not just as a response to working parents' need for childcare. The Danish perspective is more one of assessing the needs of families rather than placing day care as a consequence only of maternal employment, which is the basis for discussion in many other European countries. In theory, all parents have a right to chose a place for their child within the available early years provision and attending early years settings is seen as a normal part of childhood in Denmark.

Along with Sweden, Denmark has the highest rate of employed mothers in the EU and the numbers have risen through the last decades of the twentieth century. In 1993 76% of mothers of children 0–10 years were employed outside the home. About 80–90% of all mothers are employed and the majority of the group (65%) were in full-time employment. The vast majority of families in Denmark therefore either have an employed lone parent or two working parents. So policies to support working parents are viewed as support for the typical Danish family and not a minority part of social needs.

Regulations on leave have been extended for fathers as well as mothers. The 28 weeks of maternity leave (4 weeks taken before the birth) can, in the last ten weeks of leave be taken by either parent. Fathers also have a right to two weeks of paternity leave. Each parent is entitled to a period of 3–12 months of childcare leave, with a flat rate of payment, which can be taken at any time until the child is nine years old. In total the Danish system gives families up to 30 months of maternity plus parental leave after the birth of each child. Some of the leave depends on the employer's agreement and all is paid, although at a flat, non-earnings related rate.

Statutory education

Primary schooling

Education is free in Denmark and children start **Folkeskole** at seven years of age, although there have been some discussions about lowering the age to six years. The Folkeskole is the basic comprehensive school system covering nine years of compulsory education and a voluntary tenth year. Most Danish children pass through the state school system, about 12% going to private schools.

Danish schools close at around lunchtime or soon after, so out-of-school provision is an issue for families to cover afternoons as well as before school starts in the morning. In Denmark the difference between school holidays for children and average annual leave for employed parents is about 7–8 weeks.

Out-of-school provision

Out-of-school provision is called generally **fritid** (meaning free time). Parents make a contribution towards the cost of out-of-school care and the municipalities cannot ask for more then 20–30% of the cost from parents. From the mid 1990s out-of-school provision has been given a priority with local municipalities being required to draw up plans for out-of-school and leisure facilities for older children and young people.

The plans are required not only to be responsive to local parents but also to give a clear voice to the wishes of children and young people and to involve them in the planning of facilities. This development is a reflection of Danish policy that children should be given the opportunity to express their views and that adults should listen.

This service is offered through a range of settings. The school-based services are the responsibility of the Ministry of Education and have to follow the same rules as the Folkeskule. However, provision outside schools falls under the responsibility of the Ministry of Social Affairs. The range of provision includes:

▶ **Fritidshjem** (meaning free time homes) cater for school age children up to fourteen years in some separate centres and run from 1–00 p.m. when many, although not all, schools shut for the day. Staff are qualified paedagoger.

▶ **Skolefritidsordninger** (school based free time schemes) offer school-based care and leisure facilities for school aged children up to fourteen years. There is a trend towards locating out-of-school provision on school premises. The programme of both forms of out-of-school provision places an emphasis on creative and cultural activities and spending as much time outdoors as possible.

▶ The **aldersintegrerede institutioner** offer provision within the school.

▶ **Fritidsklubber (**free time club**)** or just **klubber** are leisure clubs open for seven to ten year olds, sometimes up to fourteen years. The clubs are open for short periods of time and operate a drop-in system. Staff are qualified paedagoger who additionally have skills in other fields such as creative activities.

In 1995 the ECNC reported that almost two-thirds of children aged six to ten years attended some kind of publicly funded centre for their age group. 24% of the age group attended fritidshjem or aldersintegrerede institutioner and 38% attended the school-based skolefritidsordninger.

6

Finland

National background

Geographical location

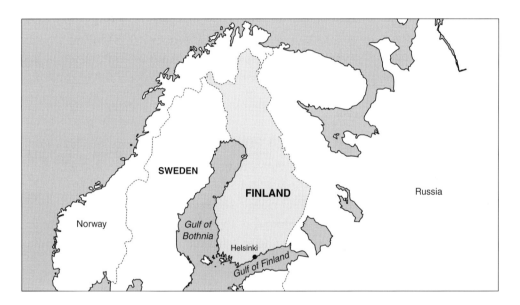

Located in the most northern part of Europe, Finland has a third of its land lying north of the Arctic Circle. It has borders with Sweden in the north-west, Norway in the north and a longer land border with Russia in the east. Finland also has a long coastal boundary to the Gulf of Bothnia in the west and the Gulf of Finland in the south.

The country is heavily forested and with a considerable number of lakes and rivers. Finland's inland waters take up almost 10% of its total area. The country is generally low lying, with most of the country no higher than 180 metres (600 feet) above sea level. Finland includes some islands as well as the mainland area. Finland's weather varies from relatively mild in the south to severe and long winters in the north.

Politics and government

Finland gained its independence in 1917 having been previously under either Swedish or Russian rule over a number of centuries.

The country now operates as a multiparty republic in which the four main political parties usually form a coalition government. Parliament is led by the President who is elected separately from the members of parliament. The Council of State is responsible for the general government of the country, although the provinces and municipalities are responsible for local government.

There is a trend towards decentralisation and to delegation of responsibility from central government to the local authorities. This move gathered in force through the 1990s when there was a significant transfer of powers from central government to the local authorities on how they developed and ran services for young children.

Social and economic framework

Finland has a developed free-market economy with state ownership of a few key industries. It was amongst the wealthiest countries in Europe but Finland has experienced serious economic recession and high levels of unemployment. This situation is shared with some other EU countries, but for Finland this has been especially linked with the collapse of its neighbour, the Soviet Union.

In common with the other Scandinavian EU countries, Denmark and Sweden, Finland has a strong tradition of state-provided social welfare and health care. The serious economic recession has placed a strain on development of services.

Finland joined the EU in 1995, at the same time as Sweden and Austria.

LANGUAGE

Finland has two main official languages: Finnish, which is a Finno-Ugric language, spoken by most of the population and Swedish, spoken by about 10% of the population as a first language, although the proportion is declining. In bilingual areas of Finland, road signs and shopfronts are in both Finnish and Swedish. Swedish has some commonality with the other Scandinavian languages of Danish and Norwegian, whereas Finnish has completely separate linguistic roots and is closest to Hungarian of all the European languages.

The Sami, with a population of several thousand, live in the far north of the country, in the region known to outsiders as Lapland, although the Sami themselves call the area Samiland. They speak a different language of Finno-Ugric origin (Sami, although sometimes called Lapp) and some families still follow a nomadic life. The Sami are a people whose traditional lands cross national boundaries to form an area including parts of northern Finland, Norway, Sweden and Russia. Local authorities are obliged to provide provision for Finnish children in the appropriate language: Finnish, Swedish or Sami.

POPULATION

In 1998 Finland had a population of 5.2 million, of whom 19% were under 15 years of age, a decline in that part of the population from 30% in 1950. Finland's fertility rate in 1993 was 1.81. The population is concentrated in the southern third of the country and especially along the southern coast.

URBAN-RURAL

Finland is the most sparsely populated country in the EU. However, within the whole continent of Europe, both Norway and Iceland have lower populations in proportion to the country's land size. Industrialisation in Finland led to migration from rural areas and three-fifths of the population now live in cities or towns. The urban shift came later to Finland than many EU countries and is reflected in a strong wish for many Finns to spend time in the countryside. Many families have summer homes outside the towns.

Pre-school provision

Finland, like its Scandinavian neighbours, has developed an integrated system of early years provision which is the responsibility of the social welfare departments, but without the overtones of children in need that accompany this pattern in some other EU countries.

Early years provision has a long tradition in Finland, starting at the end of the nineteenth century and following the Froebel approach, which is still a strong influence. Finland now has a well developed system of publicly funded centres and family day care provision. The country is unusual in the EU for offering a legal entitlement to a childcare place from birth to three years for any parents who wish to work or study. The place can be in a centre or family day care. Alternatively, parents are given a childcare allowance if they prefer to care for their child at home. The Childcare Act of 1990 was a reaction to the high employment rate of mothers of young children and concerns about the quality of private and non-regulated family day care.

Most of the early years provision is organised by the local authority who can buy in privately-run services, but usually manage their own. Only about 5% of publicly funded provision is run by private organisations. There has been a move to decentralise responsibility with the result that some regulation and responsibility for funding, management and monitoring of services has been transferred from the national to the regional authorities.

Combined day centres

Päiväkoti are early childhood centres attended by children from birth up to seven years of age. Most of the centres are run by the local authorities but some are run by private organisations. The centres are the responsibility of the Ministry of Social Affairs and Health. Parents pay fees related to family income and number of children.

The centres are organised around the concept of parent and community oriented educare. The curriculum tends to be influenced by the Froebel tradition and now more usually has mixed age groups of children, although a split at three years used to be more common. Some centres and schools stress the importance of outdoor experience, including the forest and countryside, in a similar focus to the Danish forest kindergartens (see page 71) and similar schemes dating from the 1950s in Sweden. The aim is additionally that six year olds are helped in the transition to school at seven years and some settings provide after-school care for older children. Some centres offer a broader base of family services available to the local community.

Where possible the aim is to integrate disabled children into mainstream provision, on the basis of allocating two day care places to one disabled child. Sometimes part of a centre may be reorganised to provide for children's special needs.

The adult-child ratios tend to be one trained adult to four under threes and to seven over threes. In part-time places the ratio can be 1:13.

In 1994 about 63% of publicly funded places for under sevens were in centre based care and the rest in family day care (see page 82). Centres tend to be more available in urban areas and the number of centre places has increased. In 1994 21% of children from birth to three years were in publicly funded services, about 53% of them in centres and the rest in family day care. In 1994 43% of three to seven year olds were in services within the welfare system, 64% of them in centres and the remainder in family day care.

WORKFORCE

The pattern of training for early years came under review in the second half of the 1990s. There has been a general trend away from specific training schemes and a central regulation of vocational training. It seems likely that a completed apprenticeship of any kind will be important and that the employing organisation, including childcare and education, will be responsible for arranging more job-specific training.

Centres are usually managed by a **lastentarhanopettaja** (a pre-school or early years educator) or a **sosiaalikasvattaja** (social educator). Within the total team working with the children, which will include the manager except in larger centres, one in three staff members has to be a lastentarhanopettaja or a sosiaalikasvattaja.

The qualification for lastentarhanopettaja requires a three-year training course that from 1995 has to be at university level and there are discussions about linking the training with primary school level. The training to be a sosiaalikasvattaja takes place at a tertiary level college and has a more family and social work emphasis than the heavier academic focus now part of training to be a lastentarhanopettaja.

The staff team of the full-day centres are usually **lähijoitaja** (community care workers) who have a broad based training in social care with some attention to childcare and play. Staff who trained before 1994 will have followed a different course, with more emphasis on health care, to become a lastenjoitaja (more like a paediatric nurse).

Lastentarhanopettaja can take additional specialist training to enable them to be employed to work with disabled children. They may then be called **Erityislastentar-hanopettaja**.

In some centres the pattern tends to be that the sosiaalikasvattaja (social care trained staff) work more with the younger children and the lastentarhanopettaja (qualified pre-school educators) with the older ones.

OTHER KINDS OF PROVISION

Other forms of early years provision include:

> ▶ There are some drop-in centres for family day carers, parents and children who are cared for within their own family. Such centres usually have a qualified educator who offers activities for the children. There are often workshops available for the family day carers and parents.
> ▶ Rural areas are sometimes served by mobile kindergartens which offer sessions, usually for the five to seven year olds.
> ▶ Some six year olds attend a pre-school class attached to a day care centre or school.
> ▶ Sessional playgroups – see page 84.

Family day care

Perhepäivähoito also known as **familjedagvård** is a system of family day care provided for children from birth to seven years. Individual arrangements are made between the carer and the family but the local authorities are responsible for the regulation of the service. Most perhepäivähoitaja (family day carers) are employed by the local authorities and any privately employed carers have to have a licence. About 42% of the cost of the care is met by funds from national government or the local authorities and parents pay a contribution related to family income.

Carers are regulated over how many children they can take: a maximum of four children under school age including the carer's own and a fifth child of school age. Family day carers are given compulsory training. Carers are also regularly supervised by a **perhepäivähoidonohjaaja**, who will have trained as a lastentarhanopettaja (kindergarten teacher) or have a social welfare degree. Since 1994 the training for the carers has been integrated into that for the lähijoitaja (community care workers in centres).

As an alternative to family day care in the provider's home, or care in the child's own home, Finland has a third model of **ryhmäperhehoito**, in which two or three family day carers work together. Children and the carer spend one week in each family home on a rotating basis. Some family day care is also organised in groups as two or three carers jointly look after the children on premises provided by the local authority.

Family day care is a more usual form of provision in the rural areas, whereas centres are more common in cities. In the national statistics six year olds in family day care are not counted as receiving any form of pre-school education.

Family obligations and employment

Compared with many other EU countries, Finland has a high level of full-time employment of women with children. Industrialisation came later to Finland than many other EU countries and by the 1960s there were substantial population movements as people migrated to the industrial centres of the south. The urban population expanded rapidly and the increased employment of mothers led to substantial problems in finding day care.

Finland has a parental leave system, of 263 weekdays of paid leave in which the mother has to take the first 105 days but either parent can take the remaining time. If both parents are employed, one is entitled to work shorter days until the end of the child's first year in school. A home care allowance is also available if a parent chooses to stay at home with the child. Either parent is legally entitled to three years of unpaid leave without losing his or her job. The value of paid benefits for parents has fallen in the economic recession and the choice to take time off to be with children has become more limited.

An early years group enjoy natural history

In 1993 63% of mothers with 0–10 year olds were working, only 8% of them part-time. By the mid-1990s the economic recession and resulting unemployment changed the situation in Finland. Cuts in public spending had led to a shortage of day care places. However, loss of jobs, which seemed especially to impact on women meant that there was no longer any apparent shortfall. The Finnish economy is beginning to look more positive, so the situation may change again.

Playgroup movement

Finland has a strong tradition of **päiväkerho** (playgroups) which was established after 1945 by the Lutheran Church. Attendance is open to families whether or not they attend the Lutheran church. Although regular national church attendance is low, the Lutheran playgroups are an integral part of provision in Finland. About 90% of the population are members of the Lutheran church on paper and pay church taxes.

Playgroups are staffed by **lastenohjaaja** who are trained in the Lutheran colleges. Courses are usually full-time and last two and half years. The training is similar to that of the lähijoitaja but with an additional emphasis on religious development and pastoral care.

Playgroups operate on a sessional basis and so, on their own, are not offering childcare suitable for working parents. Mostly children from four to six years attend, although younger children and some school age children may attend. Over 60% of four to six year olds attend one of the many playgroups and this proportion seems high because many children who come to playgroup are also in the care of a family day carer or may be visiting from a full-day centre.

Statutory education

Transition between pre-school and school years

A general concern to link the pre-school provision with the primary school years led to the concept of **learning modules** for five and six year olds in day care centres and schools. This pre-primary schooling, called **esiopetus**, may be provided in a päiväkoti or within school.

Some schools offer pre-school education on site, which is then free to parents. This provision is the responsibility of the Ministry of Education. This pre-school experience may be offered to children in separate classes or in combined classes along with children from the first two years of compulsory schooling. In 1994 55% of six year olds received pre-primary schooling, most of them (94%) in päiväkoti rather than schools.

Primary schooling

Children start compulsory school at seven years in Finland, although since Finland's entry into the EU there has been some discussion about lowering it to six years of age. Compulsory education is free and lasts for nine years. The majority of Finnish children gain their education through the state comprehensive system or **peruskoulu**.

Finnish schools tend to complete the school day at lunchtime or soon after. However, children are provided with lunch and supervised during this time. Children's school hours rise slightly after their first two years in school. The difference between school holidays and the average annual leave of employed adults is 8 weeks.

Out-of-school provision

There is some regulated provision but not much and most of the facilities are unregulated. During the 1990s attention turned to out-of-school provision in Finland. The funding that was allocated earlier for local authorities to develop children's services had tended to be used in provision for young children since public pressure was greatest for this age group. An increasing attention focussed on out-of-school provision but was then disrupted by the economic recession. Development may restart.

Play activities for school age children, known as **leikkitoiminta** or **lekaktiviteter** may take place in playgrounds, in the Lutheran playgroups, within family day care or in **avoin päiväkoti** or **öppen förskola** (open pre-school centres) The availability of out-of-school provision is mainly limited to these kinds of centres. In 1994 about 5% of seven to nine year olds had a place in publicly funded out-of-school provision, slightly less than half in family day care.

Municipal playspaces exist on a local basis in which outdoor playspace is made available with supervised indoor activities. This provision is not strictly offered as out-of-school care, although families often use it to that end. Children younger than four years have to be accompanied by an adult. The play staff may be unqualified although some will have completed the training for staff in the full-day centres, be youth workers or other individuals able to offer experience in crafts or sport. There are no required ratios for adults to children in the out-of-school provision.

7

France

National background

Geographical location

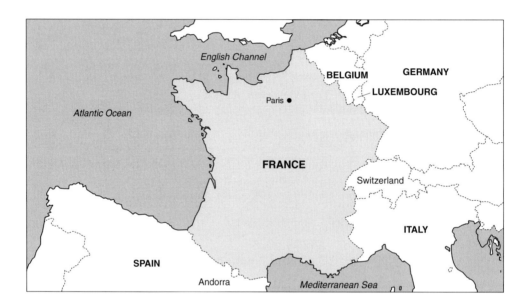

Located on the western side of the European mainland, France has land borders in the north-east with Belgium and Luxembourg, in the east with Germany, Switzerland and Italy and in the south with Spain and Andorra. In the north-west, the stretch of sea known to the English as the English Channel and to the French as La Manche divides the two countries. The Bay of Biscay section of the Atlantic lies to the west and the Mediterranean Sea to the south.

France consists mainly of the one large land mass. Monaco on the south coast operates independently, but the island of Corsica (to the south of France and west of Italy) is politically part of France.

About two-thirds of France is lowlands, with heights no more than 300 metres (1000 feet). However, some of the more mountainous regions, especially those forming the boundaries between France and Spain in the south and with Switzerland in the east, can reach close to 5000 metres (nearly 16 000 feet).

Politics and government

France is a republic with a multiparty democratic system led by an elected President. The current system was established in the 1958 Constitution of the Fifth Republic.

Paris (the capital) is the largest urban conurbation of the country. Government efforts to decentralise have been made difficult by the politically and culturally central nature of Paris and the fact that about one-fifth of the population live in or near the city. The country's rail and road links are also organised with Paris as the hub.

Social and economic framework

France is one of the larger EU countries both in land mass and population. It is one of the major economic world powers, ranking alongside the United States, Japan and Germany. Manufacturing and services are important but agriculture, although it occupies a noticeable proportion of land, is not a major part of the economy.

France was one of the original six countries that in 1958 formed what would become the EU.

LANGUAGE

The population mainly speaks French and this is the official national language. However, there is a small group of Breton speakers in the north-west, whose language has common roots with other Celtic languages such as Welsh and Gaelic. Some regions also have speakers of Occitan, Basque and German. Foreign-born workers have brought a range of languages including those from north Africa, where France had former colonies.

POPULATION

The birth rate in France fell dramatically within the twentieth century, partly as the result of the losses of two world wars. National policy has been to encourage larger families. In 1998 France had a total population of 58.8 million, of whom 19% were under fifteen years of age. In 1993 the fertility rate was 1.65.

Urban-rural

Most of the major industries are on the east side of the country, with the western section being relatively less developed. The shift to the cities has been reversed to a limited extent by migration of young people to rural areas of Provence or the Massif Central in a conscious choice to leave urban living. However, France remains a country with many rural and sparsely populated areas. Of the 36 000 communes (the smallest local unit of government) 32 000 are categorised as rural. Two-thirds of the area of France is categorised as 'deep rural', which means an average population density of only fifteen people per square kilometre.

Pre-school provision

In France children start compulsory schooling at six years. The country has a long tradition of early childhood education that started in the early part of the nineteenth century and became part of public provision in 1881. However day care is a separate system from early years education.

Day care centres

The childcare system is aimed at the under threes. There is an overlap between the age boundary of the care system and that of the early years education system starting at two and a half years. Childcare is the national administrative responsibility of the Ministry of Social Affairs. The local social service and health authorities are responsible for inspection.

The **crèches collectives** are open for children from two months to three years of age. They offer a full-day, year-round service and their objectives are usually to foster group communication and social relationships. Parents pay fees, usually related to household income.

Crèches are managed by a **puéricultrice** who also responsible for a group of children. The puéricultrices are paediatric nurses or midwives who have completed an additional year of training to extend their understanding of children and families. At least half of the staff team must be **auxiliaires de puériculture**. Both these kinds of training are more paramedical.

In centres with more than forty places at least one member of staff must be a qualified **éducatrice/éducateur de jeunes enfants,** whose training at specialist centres has an educational content. However they are not professeurs (teachers) and do not work within the educational system.

Further training for work with disabled children leads to a qualification as an **éducateur spécialise** or **moniteur-éducateur** (the assistant level).

There is now an increasing tendency in childcare settings to look for staff with a more educational than paramedical background. Some éducatrices now apply for manager positions in crèches that used only to be open to the puéricultrices.

Settings have to produce a **projet d'établissement** which describes the educational and cultural approach of the service and how parents can become involved. Staff-child ratios are one adult to five children who are not yet walking and one adult to eight older children (up to three years of age).

OTHER FORMS OF PROVISION

Parents' dissatisfaction with the paramedical emphasis of the traditional crèches has led to some alternative, parent-run **crèches parentales**. These settings increased in the last decades of the twentieth century, for instance from 1630 places in 1986 to 5600 in 1990. The crèches are subsidised by the state and run an all-day, all-year-round service. Parents sometimes work with the children alongside the staff team. The managers are usually qualified as éducateur de jeunes enfants because parents prefer the more educationally oriented and trained staff for their children's crèches than the puéricultrices of the traditional crèches.

Haltes-garderies are childcare centres that do not require that parents are working in order to get a place. These settings tend to offer sessional places and about half of them are managed by the local authorities. In principle these centres are for children from birth to six years but in practice they are mainly used for children under three years of age. The haltes-garderies were originally used by women who were not working but wanted their children looked after for a few hours a week. However, the settings are increasingly being used for regular part-time care.

Because of the varied pattern of places it is not unusual that the number of children attending over the week is considerably higher than the number of places. The European Commission Network on Childcare (ECNC) estimated that each halte-garderie place is used on average by five children.

Jardin d'enfants have developed for children from two to six years of age and their conditions tend to vary with local needs, although they can be full-day and all-year-round services. They are the combined responsibility of the Ministry of Social Affairs and the local social services but are usually managed by private organisations. It is not a common form of provision in France.

The pattern of services for French under threes makes interpretation of the available statistics more complicated. It would appear that up to half of children under three are cared for by their mothers, even though some of these parents are also employed. In 1993 the ECNC estimated that about 20% of under threes were in some form of publicly funded service. However, more than half of these places were for two year olds in écoles maternelles, which do not offer hours relating to day care (see page 92). Of the remaining group about two-thirds were attending crèches and the rest in family day care.

Family day care

Family day carers are called **assistantes maternelles** and are allowed to take up to three children. They may operate as single carers but can be organised into grouping of 30 to 40 carers to form a **crèche familiale** which is subsidised to a level of about 64% by public funds. The group is supervised by a qualified worker, usually a puéricultrice. The family day carers are expected to complete a training programme within five years of working as a carer.

The assistantes maternelles usually offer full childcare for the under threes and care for older children to close the gap between adult working hours and those of the écoles maternelles and schools. The carers can be responsible for no more than three children, including their own. In the rural areas of France, family day care, with some mixed age centres, is the most likely option for care of the under threes.

The **relais assistantes maternelles**, centres for family day carers, aim to improve the quality of a local service and to encourage contact between carers and parents.

Family obligations and employment

The main criteria for places in the crèches is that parents are working, although places are sometimes made available for children deemed to be at risk. In 1993 62% of mothers with children aged under fifteen years were employed and 69% of them worked full-time. In France generally the level of maternal employment, especially full-time, increases as a family's youngest child gets older. Women in rural areas of France have employment rates similar to women in urban areas and where they are mothers of young children, the childcare options can be limited.

During the 1990s France experienced the same economic downturn as many other EU countries and higher levels of unemployment and poorer economic conditions became a national issue. However, during the same decade, there was a steady increase in provision for childcare and out-of-school care services that supported the needs of working parents.

Earnings-related maternity leave is given for 16 weeks with the first and second child, but 26 weeks for any more children in the family. There is some level of parental leave up to a child's third birthday. Workers are allowed three days of leave per year to care for a sick child under sixteen years, which is increased to five days if there are three or more children in the family.

The Law on the Family 1994 improved parental leave and made some provisions to ease funding of services. Pre-primary schooling is free but parents receive some financial help through tax relief and some allowances for services that charge fees. The 1994 legislation explicitly favoured care for young children at home or with a family day carer. The national policy is more one of reducing overall unemployment by encouraging mothers to remain out of the labour market and care for their children at home, supported by some financial incentives.

Early childhood education

CYCLES OF LEARNING

The Law on Educational Orientation in 1989 brought about changes in the overall framework for pre-primary and primary schooling. The écoles maternelles, for children from two and half to six years, became an integral part of an educational system for children from two to eleven years, all under the responsibility of the national Ministry of Education.

The cycles of learning framework regroups the ages as follows:

1 **One:** *cycle des apprentissages premiers* (early learning) includes lower, middle and upper sections of the école maternelle, the two to five year olds. Through this period there is an emphasis on social, emotional and cognitive skills.

2 **Two:** *cycle des apprentissages fondamentaux* (basic learning) concerns the upper section of the école maternelle and the first two years of elementary school, five to eight years. This period starts to focus on literacy and numeracy. Cycles one and two deliberately share the five to six year old age range.

3 **Cycle three** covers the last three years in primary school and focusses on consolidation of children's literacy and numeracy skills.

The aim has been to strengthen the links between nursery and primary school and to ease transitions, along with avoiding repetition for children in their educational programme.

The reservations of some French early years practitioners are about losing a specific nursery educational perspective and a possible loss of contact between nursery education and other pre-school services. There is also a concern that there may be an increasingly formal approach to early learning and that play and creativity will be pushed to one side. Some écoles work to ease the transition of children into the primary school by offering some activities jointly with children in the first or second year of school.

PRE-SCHOOL SETTINGS

The early educational settings are called **écoles maternelles**, a term used since the end of the nineteenth century. By 1989 all three to five year olds were guaranteed by law a place in an école maternelle and the level of provision for three to five year olds is the highest in EU countries.

Two year olds may attend a crèche or an école maternelle, since the two forms of provision bridge this age range. In 1993–4 an average of 35% of two year olds were attending an école maternelle but there were wide regional differences. Almost all children over three years attend and both these figures have been stable for about fifteen years.

The admission of two year olds to the écoles maternelles has attracted some criticism, on the grounds that the staff are not trained for this young age group and that young children should be at home with their mothers. Supporters of the move argue for the advantages of early educational input, especially for children in deprived areas and it is in such areas of the country, the **zones d'éducation prioritaires**, that most of the places for two years old are available.

The regional differences in entry of the two year olds also seem to reflect the local child population in that two year olds are more likely to be encouraged to join the écoles when numbers would not otherwise support a full local école with its existing staff. Proportions of local two year olds can vary from, for instance, 50% in Brittany to as low as 20% in Paris.

Attendance is free in the state run écoles, which form the majority of the provision. The few private settings receive state subsidies and parents pay fees. The avowed aim of the écoles is to prepare children for primary school life, to encourage social relationships and to enable children to learn how to learn. The écoles do not usually offer close parent involvement in the settings.

ORGANISATION

The national ministry controls the organisation and the broad curriculum content of pre-school education. In the second half of the 1990s there was a move towards being more specific about curriculum content and methods to span the pre-school and early school years. A local inspector ensures that guidelines are followed, both in the state écoles and grant-aided private settings. The local authorities, the départements, own and maintain the buildings and equipment. A school council provides advice about daily running of the écoles.

Most EU countries have less provision for younger children

The écoles maternelles follow the local school hours and days, which can vary slightly between regions and they close for the same school holidays as the primary school system. The écoles are usually settings separate from schools and are especially available in urban areas. Some are part of primary schools, operating as the nursery classes of the establishment but otherwise like the separate écoles. The hours of the écoles do not meet childcare needs of working parents and some in urban areas are linked with a garderie that makes up the necessary hours for the children.

Generally children are divided into age groupings: the *petite* section of two to four year olds, *moyenne* section of four to five year olds and *grande* section for six year olds. There is some flexibility for placement of children, depending on their maturity. The ratio is an average of one teacher to about thirty children but this group will probably also have an assistant.

In rural areas with few children, it is more frequent that children are brought together in one class in which their ages span the pre-school and early school years. Some communes in rural or mountainous areas have developed a cooperative system of bringing together children from more than one commune to form a large enough group for an **école maternelle intercommunale**. Part-time pre-school education and mobile classrooms are other approaches for sparsely populated regions.

WORKFORCE

All these settings have an explicitly educational perspective. The staff are **professeurs des écoles** (teachers), with a university degree and a two-year professional qualification for working with pre-primary and primary aged children. Teachers may be supported by assistants, **agents spécialises d'école maternelle**, who are recruited by the local authorities on the basis of their own criteria.

Statutory education

Primary schooling

Compulsory schooling lasts from six to sixteen years but is closely linked with pre-primary through the cycles of learning (see page 91).

Children start compulsory education at six years but the écoles maternelles are viewed as part of the education system and operate on the same hours, days and terms as the local schools. There is a two-hour lunch break during which some local authorities provide lunch and supervision. Working parents need provision to close the gap between these settings and usual working hours. The difference between the school holidays and the average annual leave for employed adults is 11 weeks.

Out-of-school provision

French policy towards school age children and young people is implemented through specific contracts between central government and local partnerships. The contracts, developed since 1985, are within an educative framework that views children and young people as citizens with a legitimate call on local resources. The contracts include explicit recognition of care, leisure activities and sometimes issues like road safety.

There is a network of out-of-school care and recreation that is financed through national, local and voluntary sources. Nationally, these facilities come under the responsibility of the Ministry of Youth and Sport and the Ministry of Culture and Education. Services are either offered by the school management on school premises, **services périscolaires** or independently of the school, although possibly on school grounds, **services extrascolaires.**

The **garderie périscolaire** is a centre-based care for three to six year olds and sometimes older children. The garderies tend to be on existing school premises and are managed by the local authorities. The facility may include unqualified staff but may have qualified **animateurs** who have followed a training programme focussed on leisure and play for older children. The care tends to be available outside school hours but not within school holidays. Arrangements tend to be on an individual basis with parents whose children attend the école maternelle. These centres are the national responsibility of the Ministry of Social Affairs.

The **centres de loisirs sans hébergement** are care and recreation centres for two to seventeen year olds, but they are mainly attended by school age children. The centres may be on school grounds but are usually separate. The staff are usually qualified as animateurs. The centres cover the hours before and after school and in the holidays that are needed to close the gap to a normal working day for parents. They are the responsibility of the national Ministry for Youth and Sport combined with local authority youth and sports department. At the local level the centres are often run by private organisations. The centres have to produce a programme, **projet éducatif**, which describes their programme for the children and methods. In 1993 the ECNC estimated that there were places for about 12% of three to six year olds and about 30% of six to ten year olds.

8

Germany

National background

Geographical location

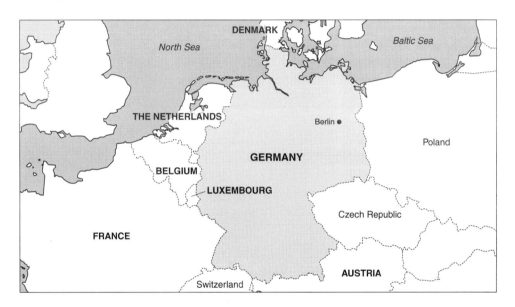

Germany lies in north–central Europe and has land boundaries on three sides. In the west, the country has borders with The Netherlands, Belgium, Luxembourg and France. Switzerland and Austria lie to the south. In the east are borders with the Czech Republic and Poland. In the north Germany has a short land border with Denmark and access to the Baltic Sea in the north east and the North Sea in north–west. Germany is mainly composed of one land mass, with only a few islands in the north.

The country is a mix of lowland with some hilly and mountainous areas.

The reunification of Germany

The current situation in Germany makes no sense without a historical perspective. During the twentieth century Germany has experienced frequent political disunity and changing national boundaries, especially following two world wars. In 1948, after the Second World War, Germany was divided into two parts and was not reunified until 1990. For decades the country operated as two completely separate halves: West and East Germany.

WEST GERMANY

The western part of Germany, known as the Federal Republic of Germany (FRG), evolved under a democratic system. The FRG developed a federal political structure as a deliberate reaction against centralisation and the excesses of the Nazi regime. The FRG was one of the original six countries who in 1958 formed what became the EU.

The country had a low employment rate for women with young children. There was substantial expansion of Kindergärten provision during the 1970s although these developments still left regional variation in the coverage. Neither childcare nor out-of-school provision was a priority and kindergärten places were often part-time. Provision for children under three years was rare and scarcely existed outside cities.

The concept of **Subsidaritatsprinzip** guides the development of services and prioritised the rights and responsibilities of individuals, voluntary bodies and the state. The practical result was that public authorities did not set up family support measures such as Kindergärtens if voluntary agencies were able to do so. The policy was that the state subsidised voluntary agencies, usually organisations run by the Catholic or Protestant churches, who then provided services.

EAST GERMANY

In contrast, East Germany, known as the German Democratic Republic (GDR), evolved under a socialist system and was part of the communist Eastern bloc of countries under the influence of the old USSR. The GDR had a centralised political structure and a high employment rate for women with young children. Involvement of women in the labour market was an expressed political goal. In response to this social and economic situation, there was an expansion of Kindergärtens to give total coverage for three to six year olds and a high provision of childcare for children under three years (higher even than in other East European countries of the time). An explicit aim of childcare and educational settings was to educate children towards the 'socialist personality'.

The hardline government of East Germany was appalled by the liberalising moves in the Soviet Union in the second half of the 1980s, but the internal pressure for reform grew steadily. The Berlin Wall (between the two parts of the city of Berlin, isolated in the East side) was physically broken down in 1989. The new government of East Germany was forced the next year to work for reunification in the face of massive migration out of the East.

The two parts of Germany were reunited in October 1990. This unification process brought together two very different political and economic systems and traditions that had developed over five decades. The old GDR joined the EU as part of a reunified Germany.

Post 1990 – politics and government

Germany as a whole nation now has a federal political structure with sixteen states or Bundesländer (known as Länder in brief). The old GDR merged into the political system established in the FRG of a democratic system with an elected president as head of state. Law making rests with the national government and the Länder are responsible for implementing legislation on a local basis and developing local policy. The Länder experience a great deal of autonomy especially in the areas of education, finance and law enforcement.

Social and economic framework

Germany is a major world trading nation and has largely recovered economically through the 1990s from the strains of absorbing the very different economy of the former East Germany.

LANGUAGE

The main and official language of Germany is German, which is also spoken in a slightly different form in both Austria and Switzerland. Within Germany there are many regional dialects, which can sound significantly different from each other. A wide range of other languages are spoken by Germany's population of foreign-born workers, the majority of whom live in the western half of the country and many of whom are from Turkey.

POPULATION

The total population in 1998 was 82.3 million, of whom 16% were under fifteen years of age. Germany has the largest population in the EU, although France and Spain have larger countries in terms of land mass.

In 1993 the national fertility rate was 1.28. However, since 1989 fertility rates have declined in the eastern Länder, in many regions by as much as 40 to 50%. Unemployment, an uncertain economic future and the closure of many day care centres seem all to have influenced the child-bearing population towards much fewer children or postponed families.

URBAN-RURAL

The western part of Germany is more densely populated than the eastern and the population is unevenly distributed in general. The capital, Berlin, is projected to have a population of about 5.5 million by 2000 and more than 11 million people live in the substantial Rhine-Ruhr industrial conglomeration where the towns and cities effectively merge one into another. About one third of the population live in the large cities but the remainder mostly live in smaller towns and villages, especially in the western part. Some parts of the country can be very rural and sparsely populated. There has also been a trend for families in the west to move out of cities so that some rural areas include peri-urban enclaves with a higher proportion of children than usual.

Pre-school provision

Unification brought together two halves of Germany who had developed different early years systems. The western part had a greater diversity of provision, including family day care but far less attention to childcare. The eastern Länder had more provision but less diversity in services. Most eastern provision concentrated on childcare, being either day nurseries (**Krippen**) for under threes or **Gantztagskindergärten** (full-day Kindergärtens) for children from three years to school age.

The Child and Youth Welfare Act 1990 created a legislative framework for all the childcare and educational services from the old east and west. Inevitably, some differences in distribution of service still remain. The 1990 Act established the importance of parental responsibility and reaffirmed the concept of **Subsidaritätsprinzip** important in the old West Germany. The approach is that of preferring any child welfare settings to be set up by private organisations and that the public authorities should only develop services in the absence of any other body. The federal government sets the legislative framework on pre-school provision, either childcare or early childhood education, but the Länder have to put the requirements into practice on a local basis.

Care and education are divided, although most services are the responsibility of the federal Ministry for Family at the national level and the social or welfare ministries in the Länder. Sometimes the local education ministries are responsible for services for three to six year olds, for instance the Vorklasse in the western Länder come under the local Ministry of Education.

In the western Länder about 70% of all the childcare and early educational services are run by voluntary agencies, mainly organisations associated with the Catholic or Protestant churches. In the eastern Länder the majority of services are run by the municipalities, only 3% by voluntary agencies and about 11% of centre based settings are workplace nurseries run by large companies. The local authority is obligated to inspect the services run by voluntary agencies.

The exact situation varies between the Länder but the different kinds of childcare and pre-school educational settings are funded from four sources: the provider of the service, contributions from parents, local municipality funds and state subsidies. In the former East Germany all the services were free to parents.

Day care centres

The differences between the old GDR and FRG in childcare still remain and the level of provision for under threes is very different between what were the two halves of the country. Day care, as well as early years education, remains more limited in the western part of Germany than in the eastern part. Day care in particular is very limited and, along with Austria, the western part of Germany provides one of the lowest levels in the EU.

Kinderkrippen offer a full-day place for children from birth to three years. They are staffed mostly by **Erzierherinnen** (who are educators but not teachers, see also page 105) or **Kinderpflegerinnen** (trained nursery workers). The Krippen have tended to move from a focus on mainly physical care towards attention to children's social needs and abilities. The shift is towards developing a specific **Krippenpädagogik**, an approach that addresses the social interaction between young children. There are no national requirements about ratios; details are decided by the Länder. In general, Krippen have a ratio of one adult to every five (or up to 7.5) under threes. Parents pay fees.

In some Länder there have been developments towards age-integrated centres for children from birth to six years and sometimes up to fourteen years. Such centres may be called **Kinderhaus** or **Familiengruppen**.

The availability of childcare has different patterns in the western and eastern Länder. In the west, Kinderkrippen and other day care centres cater for 1.8% of children under three years. Shortly before unification in 1990, the eastern part of Germany had places for 56% of children from birth to three years. This difference reflected the national policy in the East that women would be likely to work and therefore need childcare.

OTHER FORMS OF PROVISION

Some parent-managed provision, **Elterninitiative**, has been developed in some Länder. These centres usually offer much more parent involvement than the Kindergärten or Kindergrippe and hours vary according the wishes of the involved families. The centres are usually in large cities and are initiated and managed by parents. They employ paid staff but parents are often involved in the daily running in some way.

Mother and toddler groups are popular, given the lack of facilities for this younger age range, especially in the western Länder. **Speilgruppen** or **Mutterkindgruppen** offer activities where mothers stay with their children.

Family day care

Familientagespflege is the responsibility of the local Ministry of Social and Youth Affairs and the individual Länder determine the specific regulations. The **Tagesmutter** (family day carers) usually take children from birth to three years but occasionally older children too. They negotiate fees directly with parents. A Tagesmutter is self-employed and usually cares for children under school age. Another form of family day care is that of the **Pflegenester** who cares for groups of children, not in her home, but in premises rented for the purpose or made available by the local authority.

Family day care was given more status by inclusion in the Child and Youth Welfare Reform Act 1990 and now has more official recognition, especially for meeting the childcare needs of families with very young children.

Family obligations and employment

In the west, provision for the youngest children was seen as a low political priority, linked with maternal employment and families in social need, rather than as any educational opportunity. National policy in the west of the country assumed that young children would be cared for by their mothers in most families. A child allowance supports care of the child at home up to two years of age. A total of up to 30 months combined maternity and parental leave is possible for families after the birth of each child but this is not necessarily paid. Each parent is entitled to ten days paid leave per year to care for a sick child if they have a child under twelve years and 25 days if they have two or more children. Lone parents are entitled to 20 or 50 days leave.

Levels of maternal employment remain far lower in the western Länder than in the eastern. In 1993 46% of mothers of children under ten years in the western Länder were in employment but the majority (28% of this part of the female population) were in part-time work. The same social group in the eastern Länder had a 69% rate of employment with most of this group (55% of mothers of under tens) in full-time jobs. In the west, employment rates of mothers increase with the age of their youngest children, as childcare becomes a less pressing family issue.

Female employment is an issue in rural areas where, in the west, rates increased significantly through the 1980s. The employment rate for women in rural areas became 41% higher than the West German average as a whole. Some of the peri-urban regions (to which families had moved from the city) have high rates of commuting into work.

In contrast, in the eastern Länder, there has been increased unemployment in rural areas. Not all of the employed women are mothers, of course, but those who are face a significant lack of childcare, especially for under threes and out-of-school provision. Rural provision of early education through Kindergärten is also lower then for urban areas.

Early childhood education

The differences between the old West and East parts of Germany are also visible in the different distribution of early years education services. As from 1996 there has been a legal entitlement to a Kindergärten place for every child from three years to compulsory school age of six years. This was not usually a problem in the eastern Länder, but some western Länder did not have the level of provision to meet this political commitment and transition arrangements were allowed to give a deadline of 1999. There is some level of concern among practitioners about holding onto the quality of provision whilst attempting to extend the quantity.

The three years of pre-school education are separate from compulsory schooling. In the western part of Germany the policy that local authorities should ideally not run facilities created a situation in which about 70% of the Kindergärten in the west are run by private organisations, mainly churches and welfare associations. Whereas in the east the prevalent pattern was for local authorities to run the provision. From 1990 it has also been required that Kindergärten should have parents' committees, since one of the objectives of the Child and Youth Welfare Act was to increase parental participation in publicly funded services.

Despite regional differences, **Kindergärten** are a widely available form of early educational provision at which children can start at three years of age. Parents pay fees that vary between Länder. In 1994 there were places available for 73% of children between three and six and a half in the western Länder although this figure is an average and there is variation between regions. 96% of the same age group were able to have a Kindergärten place in the eastern part. The eastern Länder prior to unification had such coverage of Kindergärten that in 1990 supply of places exceeded demand.

The hours of the Kindergärten vary between areas, some offering sessions to children and some a full-day, either with a mid-day break or all the way through with mid-day meal provided. There have been some attempts to extend the hours of Kindergärtens to meet the needs of families. Parents pay fees.

The Kindergärtens do not run like a pre-primary facility in either the French or Belgian model, but follow more of a family and community-oriented philosophy. During the West German expansion of the provision during the 1970s a specific educational approach evolved called **Situationsansatz**, which sought to enable children to learn through a situation-oriented approach. Activities are less structured and teacher-centred than in French or Belgian settings. The aim is to focus on real life situations as a way to enable children to gain in social competence, skills and knowledge.

The 1990 Act created broad guidelines for the curriculum but local authorities and individual Kindergärten have the main responsibility for deciding on educational philosophy and approach. Generally the Kindergärten aim to provide a supportive social environment in tune with Situationsansatz as well as prepare children for school. Workers and provision in the eastern Länder have had to adjust to the less prescriptive western pattern for the curriculum for young children.

The adult–child ratio varies between the Länder. In the western regions the ratio could be anything from one adult to 10–14 children. In the eastern regions the ratio is more often one adult to 12–18 children. Generally at least one adult per group must be educationally qualified and second staff members in a group are assistants.

Some Länder have developed **Kindertagesstätten**, which are care facilities for children from four months to school age. There is an ongoing debate, fuelled by the differences highlighted by unification, about hours of opening, the content of the educational programme and partnership with parents and the local community.

The **Vorklassen** provide morning only sessions for five year olds in some of the western Länder. These Vorklassen come within the school system and are free to parents. They aim to prepare children for school and in some regions to help children of school age who are having adjustment difficulties. **Schulkindergärten** are a one-year specialist referral class available for children who it is thought may have difficulties in adjusting to school.

Some proposals suggest that Kindergärtens should be developed into age-integrated centres for children from birth to six years or from three to twelve years. Some such centres exist, mainly in Northrhine-Westfalia, and provide full-day cover. These centres are called **Altersubergreifende Tageseinrichtung**. The aim of some age-integrated centres is to provide more social contact across the ages than is now usual in the prevalence of one-child families in Germany.

There are some specialist centres, **Sonderkindergärten** for disabled children, although there has been a move towards integrating children into mainstream provision.

The early years workforce

Training schemes are varied for staff in the non-statutory childcare and educational settings and there are no nationally agreed regulations for the different schemes, although there are some general guidelines. The main responsibility rests with individual Länder who determine their own legislation, training requirements and the courses of study. The three main types of early years workers are described below.

Erzieherinnen (educators) are the most common group of workers in early years educational and childcare settings. Their three-year training at a vocational college prepares them not only to work in Kindergärtens or the Kinderkrippen (see page 101) but also with a wider age range including out-of-school care. They are not teachers, who have a separate training and career path. Erzieherinnen from the eastern Länder were trained for specific kinds of provision and have had to complete an adaptation course to extend their coverage to all the different kinds of early years and out-of-school provision.

There is an ongoing debate about the training level and content for Erzieherinnen. The events since unification have left these qualified workers in a different position in the western and eastern Länder. In the west the Erzieherinnen have seen an expansion of job opportunities. However, their colleagues in the east have experienced a narrowing of employment opportunities with a significant drop in the birth rate and a reform of the administrative system leading to closures of Kinderkrippen and Kindergärten.

Kinderpflegerinnen are nursery workers who follow a two-year training that specialises in childcare at a vocational school. The qualification used to be more directed as work in families as a nanny. However, the growth of children's centres has led the training to extend. Qualified workers are enabled to work in Kindergärten, Kinderkrippen and out-of-school care, mostly as an assistant to an Erzieherin.

Sozialpädagoginnen follow a course of four or four and a half years at a tertiary college, training alongside social workers. They are then qualified to work in childcare and early education but also services that extend to family support and more social care. The Sozialpädagoginnen often manage childcare or educational settings but they are far less prevalent as a professional worker than the Erzieherinnen.

Statutory education

Primary schooling

German children start compulsory education at six years of age when they join the **Grundschule** (basic school). They must attend the primary and then secondary stage for a total of nine or ten years (the Länder differ) and then undertake a further two years education either in the main secondary school or in a vocational school. Schooling is free.

The Länder have considerable responsibility for the detail of education but are expected to follow national guidelines for the curriculum and standards. Following reunification there was concern to bring some consistency to the educational systems of west and east.

The school day finishes at lunchtime or soon after and most schools do not provide lunch. The school day can vary within the week.

Out-of-school provision

The prevailing assumption in the west is that children should be able to return home to spend the afternoons with their mother. In much the same way as with day care, the impression remains that services are needed mainly for problem families. The eastern part of Germany has far greater out-of-school provision, reflecting the different policy historically towards mothers in employment. The difference between school holidays and the average annual leave for employed adults is nine weeks.

In 1994–5, out-of-school provision was available for 5.6% of six to ten year olds in the west but for 60% in the eastern Länder. The consequence is that mothers in the western regions tend to seek part-time work, although these hours still do not necessarily fit easily with school days and holidays.

Provision for children needs peaceful areas as well as activity

There are some established centres, the **Kinderhorte**, which offer places for school age children before and after school hours. Children attend up to ten years, or sometimes twelve or fourteen. The aim of programmes of activities is more of a youth work focus than on school-type activities. The ratio is usually about one adult to 12 to 18 children and normally one member of staff for a group is qualified, as an Erzieherin or Sozialpädagogin.

The **Horte**, a centre separate from school, is the most common form of provision within the limited availability in western Germany. Just over half are managed by the local authorities and the rest by private organisations. There have been some school based Horte, known as **Schulekinderhauser** (school children's houses) in which support for homework can be a key feature and the provision does not necessarily continue through the school holidays. Since all school children have homework from six years old, time and quiet to complete their tasks is a usual part of Horte activities before free play.

In eastern Germany provision **Schulhorten** (school-based services) were developed in which children were usually looked after during out-of-school hours by their own teacher. This provision has continued, although it has moved to the responsibility of the local youth services rather than education. Most of the Horte are managed by local authorities, although private organisations are increasingly taking a role.

9

Greece

National background

Geographical location

Greece is the most southern of the European countries on the Balkan Peninsula. It is a country characterised by mountains and islands and it is hard to be far away from one or the other in any part of the country. Mainland Greece has less than a fourth of its land mass as lowlands and the rest can be mountainous, the highest peak being 2917 metres (9570 feet). The mainland is in two parts, divided by the Corinth Canal that has made the southern section, the Peloponnese, technically an island.

Greece includes more than 2000 islands, of which 170 are inhabited, and which comprise one-fifth of Greece's total land area. Crete is the largest of the Greek islands, stretching about 165 miles from west to east. Some islands lie to the west of the Greek mainland, some within the south and east of the

Mediterranean surrounding much of the country and some far to the east close to Turkey, with whom Greece has a long history of fraught political relations, including periods of occupation. Greece's land borders include Albania, Macedonia (part of the old Yugoslavia; a neighbouring Greek region is also called Macedonia) and Bulgaria along the northern boundary and Turkey in the east.

Politics and government

During the twentieth century Greece has experienced times of political instability and authoritarian regimes including a military coup in 1967. Democracy was restored in 1974 and the 1975 Constitution established a republic with a parliamentary democracy. At the same period a referendum ended the Greek monarchy's role in national government. Since then a series of democratically civilian governments have followed one another, sometimes with abrupt changes. Greece has traditionally been a highly centralised political system but there is now a slow movement into decentralisation (see page 111).

Social and economic framework

Greece has a developing, mainly private enterprise economy. Although the economy is growing, the country is still one of the poorest countries in the EU. Agriculture, tourism and manufacturing are all important parts of the Greek economy.

Greece joined the EU in 1981 and was the first country from the Eastern part of Europe to do so. Gaining membership was a statement of Greece's European identity given its location on the meeting of Europe, Asia and close to northern Africa.

LANGUAGE

The main language is Greek, which has a different alphabet to other languages in the EU. The terms in this chapter are therefore the usual translations into our alphabet. Parts of Greece that are close to other Balkan countries have populations that share other languages such as Turkish.

POPULATION

In 1998 the population of Greece was 10.5 million of whom 16% were under 15 years, in contrast with 28% in 1950. The fertility rate in 1993 was 1.34.

Greece has experienced one of the lowest population growths in the southern European countries largely because of continued emigration provoked by poor economic prospects.

URBAN-RURAL

As late as the 1960s more than 40% of Greece's population lived in the mountainous areas of the country. The capital, Athens, has expanded rapidly in the second half of the twentieth century and now about third of the total population live in the city or its surrounds.

There has been significant migration out of the rural to the urban areas. Yet rural and village life is still of importance in Greece and more than a third of the population is still classified as living in rural areas. Some rural areas are especially inaccessible and sparsely populated, making service provision a difficult task. Many rural areas in Greece experience considerable levels of poverty.

Pre-school provision

Political changes

The development in the nineteenth century of Greek early years provision was influenced in two separate waves. In the middle of the century, the ideas of Carpentier were prominent, a Frenchman who stressed learning to read and write. Then in the second half of the century Froebel's ideas gained ground and influenced later developments. In 1929 training institutions were first set up for early years workers. However, from that time until the early 1980s, colleges were regularly closed and opened according to the political climate of the time, with a predictably disruptive effect on any continuity in the profession. In the mid 1980s early years training was generally upgraded to tertiary level and the length of the courses extended.

DECENTRALISATION

During the 1990s the Greek government decided to decentralise the entire administrative system and move Greece from being a highly centralised system to increasing the responsibilities of local authorities.

The national government proposed that the local authorities become far more involved in the organisation, administration and financing of all state pre-school services. Timetables and the curriculum had been nationally determined by central government, but the current aim is to shift these responsibilities to local authorities. The concept has been launched that the provision should operate for the common good to support the needs of young children and their families. Only the funding and appointment of teachers in nursery schools will remain the responsibility of the Ministry of Education. All else is to be decentralised and become the responsibility of local Social Policy Departments.

At the time of writing (1999) early childhood policies and administration in Greece are theoretically in transition. Early childhood services have traditionally been divided into two main types – the half-day nursery schools and full-day centres – and there has been some conflict between the two sectors. It is not yet possible to judge whether care and education will remain fairly separate or become more integrated over time. There are considerable regional differences in the levels of different kinds of provision and it is not possible yet to know how further local autonomy will affect existing variation. There is also some concern among Greek early years specialists about the lack of expertise at the local level to ensure the quality of provision.

Until part way through the 1990s children in Greece started school at five and half years of age but the entry is now at six years old. Prior to the start of compulsory schooling, there are two separate systems of childcare and early education. Most of the educational and childcare provision is state run, although there are some private or municipal settings. There are two different patterns of training for the two sectors.

Day care centres

All other forms of provision other than early education were the responsibility of the national Ministry of Health and Social Affairs that controlled financial and administrative matters and the appointment of staff. This responsibility should now be passing to the local authorities, although the national Ministry is expected to continue to pay staff and running costs.

The Greek term covering day care for the under sixes is **vrefonipiakos stathmos**. There are two kinds of day care centre for children open on a full-day, all-year-round basis. A **vrefikos stathmos** is a centre for children from birth to two and a half years, whereas the **paedikos stathmos** caters for children aged from two and a half to six years of age. The centres were originally developed as a service for working mothers and their management has been a local responsibility since 1995. Most centres are state run, some are private and Athens has some municipal centres.

Most of the available centres cater for the older age range and day care for children under two and a half years is less common. A few extended age centres are organised into two younger age groups and a nursery school section for the over threes. There are no national requirements about adult-child ratios but the state-run centres tend to work with 2:30. Local authorities that organise their own services tend to work with a ratio of 2:25.

The European Commission Network on Childcare (ECNC) estimated that in 1993 about 3% of children under three years of age were attending day care centres. At the same time, about 64% of children from three years of age to school age (then five and half years) were in publicly funded provision. The majority of them (76%) were attending **nipiagogia** (nursery schools) and the remainder (24%) were in full day centres or other provision within the welfare system.

The different kinds of day care centres used to be free in the state sector and a contribution to meals was related to family income. Parents paid fees to the private centres but it seems likely that locally run state centres will now charge a fee related to family income. Places are available to children from families with specific needs, such as low economic status, lone parents or children with special needs. The centres offer day care to meet the children's and parents' needs up to a day of eight or nine hours in length.

Staff in the centres include **vrefonipiagogos** or **vrefonipiokomes** (nursery educators), assistants or perhaps **nipiagogos** (nursery teachers). During the 1990s the centres faced a serious shortfall of staff as a result of financial cuts. The vrefonipiokomes are a new type of early years professional who are graduates of early childhood care and education departments of tertiary level Higher Technological Institutes (three years of study and a half year work placement). They work in the day centres, but not the nipiagogia (nursery schools), and the two systems of training are separate. Although the School Reform Act 1985 planned for the integration of early education and childcare, the model has not yet been implemented.

There is no officially required curriculum for the centres but many try to follow the general lines of the national curriculum and the approach of the nipiagogia (see page 115).

Family day care

Greece has always had informal care of children by relatives, neighbours and friends but has not had a system of organised family day care. However, the

EU programme of New Opportunities for Women (NOW) set up a training programme for potential family day carers and some experimental schemes have been tried out in urban areas. In 1992 legislation opened the possibility of family day carers being employed as part of publicly funded provision, but there seems to have been next to no development of this possibility. The few self-employed family day carers are called **miteres filoxenias**.

Family obligations and employment

From 1975 onwards an increasing number of women entered the job market, including mothers. Greece has experienced relatively high inflation and families without land can find survival difficult with only one income.

In 1993 44% of women with a child under ten years worked outside the home. Less than half of them (40%) worked on a full-time basis. A the same period 45% of mothers with a child under fifteen years were employed but the majority (93%) on a full-time basis, suggesting a shift as children became older.

There is 14 weeks maternity leave (26 weeks for the third or later children). Each parent is entitled to three months' parental leave, but since this allotment is unpaid, there is very limited take up. Parents are entitled to six days unpaid leave per year to look after a sick child of under sixteen years, increasing to eight days for families with two children and ten days for three or more children.

The range of provision for children has not been responsive to the changing role of women in Greek society. Childcare may be in theory a political priority, but childcare that is suitable for working mothers is still in short supply and many families seem to be dependent on family or informal arrangements.

Like some other EU countries, the situation is very different between the rural and the urban areas of Greece. The more rural areas and some of the islands have a falling population with the significant migration to the cities. Especially in the more mountainous districts, it can be very difficult for women to find employment or training and children can be socially isolated. Day care centres are practically non-existent and extended family care is often not available in the more remote areas.

Nevertheless employment of women in agriculture in the rural areas raises the issue of safe childcare and there is sometimes next to no provision.

Some seasonal provision can help and winter conditions in some mountainous areas make accessibility a real practical problem during parts of the year. In some areas of Greece families need the intense seasonal employment from tourism to make most of the family income for the year. The tourist months include those when Greek schools are shut and many areas have very limited day care for young children. Anecdotal evidence suggests that many families manage with informal care arrangements, including use of older siblings.

Women who work in agriculture often have to take young children with them as they work or leave them with older siblings. The location of primary schools often requires children to make long journeys, schools do not offer a mid-day meal and there is no after-school care. The private welfare association EOP has opened day care centres and some seasonal centres that operate during summer.

Early childhood education

The **nipiagogia** are nursery schools under the responsibility, to date, of the national Ministry of Education and Religious Affairs. The nipiagogia are regarded officially as part of the first level of the Greek education system. Statutory schooling starts at six years of age and a plan in the mid-1980s to make attendance at nipiagogia compulsory was not implemented.

So, the nipiagogia are still optional and in the state sector are free. Most settings are state run but some are private (about 3% of the children in nipiagogia are in a private setting). They may be in separate buildings, although some form part of a primary school. The provision is usually kept small, with one or two age-related groups, and offers educational provision for children from about three and half to school age. In 1991–2 about 20% of children between three and a half and four and a half were attending nipiagogia.

There is a growing social awareness of the needs of disabled children and their families, but integration into mainstream provision including school is still at an experimental stage.

Nipiagogia usually follow the same hours and holidays as the primary schools and so are open only on a half-day basis in the morning. Those that open for a full day usually offer sessions to different groups of children morning and afternoon. In 1997 160 full-day (8–00 to 4–00) nipiagogia were started on

Religious and other voluntary organisations are sometimes involved in provision in different EU countries

an experimental basis. The numbers of nipiagogia have been steadily increased but still do not meet the level of local demand in many areas.

The provision is run by **nipiagogos** (nursery teachers) who are graduates from the University Department of Early Childhood Education, having followed four years of study.

Up until the late 1990s, the Greek National Ministry of Education determined the national curriculum (established in 1989) including instructions for the nursery stage. This ministry is responsible for the financial and administrative functions and appointment of teachers. The aim of the nipiagogia is steadily to prepare children for school. There is a focus on children's all-round development with an introduction to early literacy and numeracy.

Statutory education

Primary schooling

Children used to start school at five and a half but this was changed in 1996 to six years of age. Schooling lasts until children are fifteen. The majority of schools are state run, with only a small number of private schools.

The schools shut at lunchtime or soon after and the length of the school day increases slightly as the child gets older. For a while some schools, especially in Athens and other large towns, offered either morning or afternoon places in order to meet the numbers of school age children in a situation of insufficient school buildings. There is some indication that mornings are now the pattern. The difference between primary school holidays and the average annual leave of employed adults is eleven and a half weeks.

Out-of-school provision

Although the authorities recognise the need for out-of-school care, there is very limited organised provision for children attending the nipiagogia or primary schools. During the mid 1990s there were some experimental schemes run by teachers in the school holidays on school premises and some schools organise some form of provision around school hours, for which parents pay a fee. Rural areas are especially badly served for any kind of out-of-school care. Such centres as exist for school age care and recreation are called **kentra imeras** but there are no reliable figures for how many children attend.

10

Ireland

National background

Geographical location

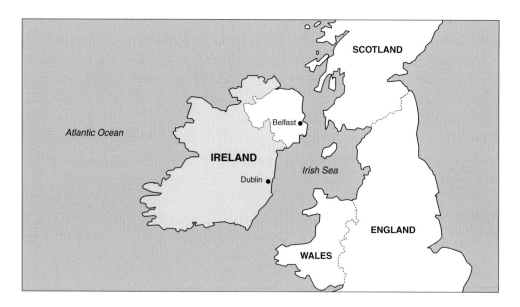

Ireland, also known by its gaelic name of Éire, occupies the greater part of an island to the west of Wales and England. Ireland shares a land border in the north with Northern Ireland, that is part of the UK. Ireland otherwise has coastal boundaries, with the Irish Sea on the east side and the Atlantic on the west. Ireland forms the most westerly part of Europe.

Ireland consists of a broad central plain ringed almost completely by coastal highlands. The plain has low elevations up to 120 metres (400 feet) and some of the mountains reach over 1000 metres (over 3000 feet). The east coast is less hilly and has the country's ports, whereas the west and south-west coastlines offer dramatic scenery as the mountains thrust directly into the Atlantic ocean.

Politics and government

There has been a strained historical relationship between Ireland and the UK, most specifically with England. Until 1922 the whole of Ireland was an integral part of the UK, at which point Éire became an independent member of the British Commonwealth. Then in 1948 Éire severed all political links to become wholly independent as the Republic of Ireland. Éire comprises all of the southern part of the island with the exception of six of the nine counties of Ulster, which became Northern Ireland and remained part of the UK.

Ireland is a republic with a democratically elected government led by the President. The vast majority of Ireland's population is Catholic and the influence of the church on national policy has historically been strong.

Social and economic framework

Ireland joined the EU in 1973 and in 1979 separated its currency from the UK pound sterling when Ireland (but not the UK) joined the European Monetary System (see page 11).

Economic links with the UK have remained close although Ireland now has strong trade links with other EU countries. There has been a steady shift from agriculture towards industry and manufacturing and the development of computer and financial services. Tourism is an important part of the economy.

The Constitution determines that the state should favour private initiative but in the absence of such moves, the government is empowered to undertake essential services and promote development projects. Ireland's economy has improved significantly towards the end of the twentieth century. The change is reflected in the fact that, when Ireland first joined the EU, the country was a net receiver of funds and now the country is economically strong enough to move towards being a net contributor.

LANGUAGE

Ireland has two main languages. Irish Gaelic is recognised as the first official language and English as the second. Irish Gaelic has many similarities with Scottish Gaelic and they are part of the same Celtic group that also includes Welsh. All official documents are published in Gaelic and English.

Gaelic was widely spoken on a daily basis up until the middle of the nineteenth century and the language then experienced a decline that has been significantly reversed in the second half of the twentieth century. Daily use of Gaelic is restricted to relatively limited Gaelic-speaking areas, called Gaeltacht, but the language is now more widely read, spoken and understood than any time since the mid–nineteenth century. English is universally spoken.

POPULATION

Historically Ireland has experienced substantial emigration, that has kept the population lower than the relatively high birth rate of a predominantly Catholic country would predict. The rate of emigration from Ireland has greatly exceeded any other EU country.

The population in 1998 was 3.7 million, of whom 23% were under 15 years of age (29% in 1950). Ireland therefore has the highest proportion of children and young people in the population of all the EU countries. However, the country now has a falling fertility rate so the proportion is likely to change in subsequent generations.

URBAN–RURAL

Ireland is a predominantly rural country and 43% of the population live in areas categorised as rural. However, a decline in agricultural employment has led to a move towards towns and cities especially from the poorer regions on the west coast.

Pre-school provision

Historically the state in Ireland has had minimal involvement in early childhood services, with the consequence that any provision for children younger than the statutory school age of six years has emerged in an unregulated way. There has been no national framework to coordinate early years care or education. The main reason has been the prevailing national policy that mothers should be at home with their children, a stance specifically included in the Irish Constitution.

The national climate has been changing and demand for services for working parents, including women, has grown. The improved economic position of Ireland has also removed the other reason given for lack of services, namely that the state had more pressing calls on the budget. EU directives have also increased the pressure for a national response to help families to reconcile home and job obligations.

In 1996 Partnership 2000 was established in which the Department of Justice, Equality and Law Reform was given the responsibility of formulating a national framework for the childcare sector. There have been some changes, although the focus still tends to be on services for young children who are deemed to be in social need rather than legitimate services for working parents.

There is a low level of publicly funded early childhood provision outside the statutory school system. Ireland has no established tradition of early years education, such as the nursery schools of many other EU countries. Any educational provision is the responsibility of the national Department of Education. Such day care provision as exists is the responsibility of the national Department of Health. This group includes any facilities that are not schools and so it covers the few day and workplace nurseries and family day care. The significant playgroup movement in Ireland is also the responsibility of the welfare system.

During the 1990s the government's aim has been to decentralise school administration and to delegate responsibility from the national Department of Education to regional Education Councils. The objective was to give opportunities for services to respond to local needs and to allow more community involvement.

The Childcare Act 1991 had a few sections relating to early childhood services, the first reference of this kind in Irish law. The 1996 regulations provide for the supervision and inspection of any pre-school services, defined as for children under six years. Services remain the responsibility of national and local welfare departments. However, one section of the Act gave Education a consultative and advisory role in pre-school services.

Day care centres

The history of provision outside the school system is that it has been viewed exclusively as a response to children who are at risk in some way because of deficits in family care.

Day nurseries are mainly private although there are some state nurseries. The **social services nurseries** are sometimes called pre-school centres or children's centres and open on a full-day, all-year-round basis. The Department of Health funds the nurseries and the regional health boards manage them. The nurseries offer places on criteria related to social and economic disadvantage and waiting lists are long. Children can attend from three months up to school age, although the youngest children are usually a year old and the eldest tend to be the four year olds, since parents then opt for pre-primary schooling.

The local health boards also use some community playgroups (see page 125) as a placement for children judged to be at risk. **Private day nurseries** offer a similar age range and opening times to the social services nurseries. Some day care centres combine full day care with a playgroup sessional facility and after-school care. Most are privately run businesses and some are franchises. There are a few **workplace nurseries**. The Irish National Children's Nurseries Association aims to promote high quality in such centres. Parents pay fees for day care.

There are no national requirements about ratios but the local Health Boards recommend for the centres they fund a ratio of 1:3 for children under a year old, 1:5 from a year up to two and half and then 1:8 up to six years.

The day nurseries are staffed by qualified **childcare workers** who have followed a two-year course. The Health Boards tend to prefer applicants with an award from the Dublin Institute of Technology. **Nursery nurses** may also be part of the team and they will have trained at a college of further education or possibly a private college. They may obtain the national Certificate in Early Childhood Care and Education, similar to the training of the childcare workers. Nursery nurses may have taken one of the UK diplomas through CACHE (see page 184). Some pre-school centres or private schools also take Montessori-trained teachers. In 1991 the National Council for Vocational Awards was established to develop a comprehensive system to cover vocational education and training programmes, not only in childcare.

Since day care is unregulated, it is difficult to obtain reliable statistics. Social services day nurseries are open for a full day and in 1991 catered for an estimated 2.6% of under fives. Private day nurseries take an estimated further 2.5% of this age group. A small number of workplace nurseries take another 0.2% of the age group. The figures are far from reliable but reflect the low level of provision.

Statistics are difficult to interpret because of the different kinds of provision included in general totals. In 1993 the European Commission Network on Childcare estimated that 2% of children under three years were enrolled in any kind of subsidised provision (not private facilities) but the centres were not necessarily offering full-day care. About two-thirds of the children attended a sessional community playgroup and about one-third had a full-day centre place. About 3% of the three to six year olds are in this range of provision, again the majority with attendance at playgroups (see page 124).

CHANGES

The pressure of demand for improved quantity and quality in early childhood provision brought about increasing change in Ireland through the 1990s. Funding, qualifications, a willingness to develop some partnership with parents have all been in a state of flux. There has also been growth in the numbers of private day nurseries.

COMPENSATORY PROVISION

From the late 1960s there have been a small number of projects that specifically aimed to support children from disadvantaged areas through the provision of early care and education, following the model of Head Start and other compensatory programmes in the United States. The Rutland Street Project in Dublin (the capital) in 1969 is usually seen as the appropriate model.

The Department of Education has funded a number of Early Start projects and in 1994 eight new pre-school centres were established, with the aim that more would follow after evaluation of the schemes. They were linked to existing primary schools in areas of designated social disadvantage. The centres were able to take up to 60 three and four year olds on a sessional basis. Each group of children had a primary school teacher and qualified childcare assistant. The aim of the innovatory programme was to combine elements of care and education for the children.

Family day care

This form of provision remains largely unregulated by the state and it is estimated to be a growing form of childcare. Family day carers are called **childminders** and are self-employed, with agreements negotiated directly with the families. The Childcare Act 1991 specifically excluded regulation for family day carers unless they took four or more children under six years of age, including their own. No training is required for childminders.

Family obligations and employment

Ireland shares with Spain the lowest employment rate for women with children within the EU. In 1993 35% of mothers of children up to ten years were in employment in Ireland. Indications are that the proportion is growing. EU funding for Ireland has exerted an impact on the debate about childcare facilities. Ireland offers up to three months of combined maternity and parental leave after the birth of a child.

However, there is a gap in maternal employment between qualified and unqualified women, with some estimates that double the proportion of qualified women holding jobs in contrast with unqualified. The practical issue is that the qualified women are better paid and therefore able to pay the costs of day care in the absence of state-subsided provision.

Paid employment of women is lower in rural than urban areas, although 1990 data suggested that a considerable number of 'farm wives' were undertaking farm-related or administrative work for no payment. The EU New Opportunities for Women (NOW) project has been one source of pressure towards development of provision and a framework for its continued growth. The work raised awareness that playgroups were usually the only form of early years provision in rural areas.

Playgroups

From the end of the 1960s a significant playgroup movement developed in Ireland in the absence of other provision for children of pre-school age. This development has a common thread with playgroup development in several other EU countries, notably the UK.

Playgroups offer sessional attendance for two or three hours and are available for children from two and a half to school age, although most children are four years and younger. Adult-child ratios can vary but tend to be one adult to between 8–10 children. Parents pay fees and the playgroup management may vary the cost depending on family income. The aims are similar to the UK playgroup movement in that activities are designed to help children learn through play and parent involvement in the group is a strong theme. The playgroups were not designed to meet the childcare needs of working parents.

In 1995 the Irish Pre-school Playgroups Association (IPPA) offered places to over 20 000 children. IPPA has a code of practice for its members and a network of regional advisers and tutors. Playgroups are the most widespread form of pre-school provision and IPPA provides some sense of quality control in the absence of government regulation. It is estimated that about 60% of the playgroups are part of IPPA and that about 5–6% of the relevant

Playgroup movements have developed in several EU countries

age group attend playgroups. Figures are estimates since not all groups are part of IPPA.

The majority of the playgroups are run by private agencies, mainly in family homes. An estimated 85% of children in Irish playgroups are in the **home-based groups**. **Community playgroups** tend to be run in local or school halls and are administered by a management committee. Although there are some state subsidies, the playgroups tend to be underfunded.

Since the late 1960s some playgroups, an estimated 218 by 1997, have offered a bilingual provision, with the playgroup leader mainly speaking Irish Gaelic. It is estimated that about 27% of children attending playgroups attend these specialist settings. The playgroups are called **Naíonraí** and are supported by the organisation An Comhchoíste Réamhscolaíochta Teo. These playgroups are also sessional and tend to take three and four year olds. Children need not be Gaelic speakers in order to attend, since the aim is to encourage learning as well as speaking Gaelic. The Naíonraí are also part of a regional network of support and training.

Early childhood education

Ireland does not have a system of separate nursery education, such provision as exists is organised within the school system.

Children in Ireland have a statutory age of six years for starting school. However, in 1993 almost all the five year olds (99%) and over half of the four year olds (55%) attended **pre-primary classes** located within the primary schools (Department of Education figures). A small number of three year olds (1%) was also in pre-primary classes. Attendance prior to six years is on a voluntary basis and children follow a curriculum determined by the Department of Education, the aim of which is to prepare them for school. The infant curriculum is designed to be more child-centred and less formal than that for older children.

Four year olds attend what is known as a **junior infant class** and the five year olds a **senior infant class**. The hours vary but usually total about 20 hours within a week. Infant classes are staffed by primary school teachers who have taken a three or four year degree course at a college of education. The class size is variable but can be as high as 35 for four year olds. In theory the ratio in the infant classes should work out as one teacher with an assistant for every fifteen children.

The infant classes follow the same school year as the primary section but are usually finished by early afternoon. Pre-primary services within the school system are free for parents and transport may also be provided in rural areas. The educational system appears to be developing a greater partnership with parents and school boards of management have been encouraged by a government circular to involve parents.

Services have also been developed to meet the special needs of children from traveller families. There are about between 40–50 pre-school units for this group of children, usually available for children from three years of age. These units tend to be run by local voluntary organisations although subsidised by the Department of Education.

Statutory education

Primary schooling

Almost all primary schools have substantial state subsidies but most are established under the patronage of the Catholic Church. There has been some demand for non–denominational schools. Schooling lasts from six years to fifteen but in practice many four and five year olds are in infant classes.

The primary school day ends mid–afternoon and the infant classes tend to finish earlier in the afternoon. Children are supervised in the lunch break and most bring a packed lunch from home. The difference between primary school holidays and the average annual leave of employed adults is 10 weeks.

Out-of-school provision

There is no organised system of care and leisure provision for children of school age and there are no reliable figures on the few schemes that exist. Most families manage through informal local arrangements between neighbours. Some nurseries and community playgroups have extended their hours to provide cover for school age children. There are a few holiday playschemes, for instance in Dublin.

11

Italy

National background

Geographical location

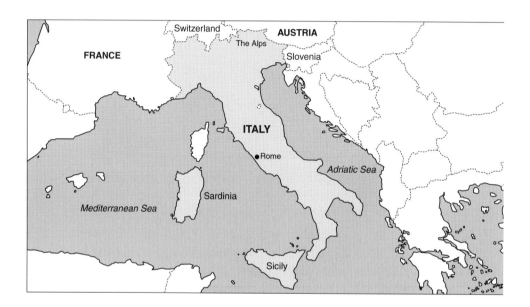

Italy forms a long peninsula with land borders in the north with France, Switzerland, Austria and Slovenia. Otherwise Italy has coastal boundaries onto various parts of the Mediterranean Sea. The islands of Sardinia in the west and Sicily in the south are also politically part of Italy and the country has some smaller islands as well.

Italy has some lowland but just 40% of the land is classified as hilly and 39% as mountainous. The Alps create a mountainous northern border, with the highest peak at 4634 metres (over 15 000 feet). The Italian landscape has historically encouraged the development of relatively independent local regions.

Politics and government

Italy is a republic subdivided into regions (regioni) which have a degree of autonomy from central government. Until the 1990s Italy had a succession of coalition governments usually led by the Christian Democratic Party, none of which were in power for very long. In 1991 there was a considerable realignment of the parties with the result that they became more clearly oriented to the political left and right. Italy was one of the original group of six countries that in 1958 formed what became the EU.

Continued political instability has meant that policies affecting childcare and early education have sometimes not been implemented. Coordination of effort, including the gathering of reliable information, has often foundered on the frequent changes in the national government structure. A lack of coherent national framework had allowed wide regional variations to persist, despite some innovatory developments that have attracted international interest.

Social and economic framework

In the second half of the twentieth century Italy experienced a rapid process of industrialisation that led to a significant move from rural to urban areas. Italy has marked differences in prosperity summarised by a north–south divide that reflects differences in economic well being and also more of a regional than national identity in some cases. The northern part of the country, with its greater industrial development, is far more prosperous than the south and the islands. Development in those poorer areas has been subsidised by the state and EU funding.

Italy has a mixed private and public economy and its public sector is one of the most extensive in the EU. Industry and manufacturing are important, as is also the tourist industry.

Language

The main language is Italian, which is spoken by the vast majority of the population. There is a small German speaking minority in the north and even smaller communities speaking French and Ladin.

POPULATION

In common with other EU countries, Italy has a low rate of increase of the population. In 1998 the population was 57.7 million, of whom 15% were under fifteen years of age (26% in 1950). Italy is experiencing a declining fertility rate, which was 1.22 in 1993. Fertility rates continued higher in the south of the country although even the more southerly regions now have declining rates. The fertility rate in northern Italy is one of the lowest in the world and many families have a single child.

URBAN-RURAL

About one third of the population live in rural areas but these regions can vary from sparsely populated and poor areas to relatively prosperous peri-urban regions to which people have deliberately moved in order to leave city life.

Pre-school provision

Early years facilities in Italy were first developed in the nineteenth century and the ideas of Froebel were influential from about the middle of that century. By the turn into the twentieth century, the ideas of Carolina and Rosa Agazzi were shaping the approach to young children. They stressed the importance of a family atmosphere and motherly qualities in the staff. The term **scuola materna** arose from their approach and is still used for Italian pre-school educational facilities. In the first decade of the twentieth century the ideas of Maria Montessori became more prominent (see also page 28). However, the Montessori centres were closed by the Fascist government of the 1930s and, with the active support of the Catholic Church, the Agazzi philosophy came to be the official approach to early childhood education.

There are two separate forms of Italian provision: early years education for three to six year olds and day care within the welfare system for the under threes. Overall there is a low level of provision for under threes.

Day care centres

Day care is offered in **asili nidi** that are viewed as a service to support families and for working mothers. The centres usually offer a full-day, all-year-round service. At the national level the centres are under the responsibility of the Ministry of Health, but the local authorities usually manage their centres through the local educational department. Parents pay for the service, sometimes at a rate that takes account of family income.

Increasingly local authorities have seen the provision as a broad based service for children's learning and socialisation and additionally for the support of children in need. There are no national standards for day care services and adult–child ratios are influenced both by national labour laws and regional agreements. The ratio tends to be one adult to six children under three years.

The European Commission Network on Childcare estimated in 1991 that there were places for about 6% of under threes to attend an **asilo nido**. It seems likely that some places are used by more than one child through part provision and a method of registering more than one child per place when there were frequent absences.

There remain significant regional differences in day care provision, in that 75% of the available places are in northern and central Italy. In some northern provinces up to 30% of under threes have a place in an asilo nido. Some parents' cooperatives have developed as a way to close the gap between demand and supply but childcare remains limited. Parents usually pay fees related to family income. Rural areas have a lower level of provision than towns for day care and also for pre-primary and primary schooling. In sparsely populated areas, and with the falling birth rate, some children have no choice but to travel to the nearest larger village or town.

Some different staff and qualification terms exist between regions of Italy. The asili nidi tend to be staffed by an **educatrice di asilo nido** who has had between three to five years training. The **puéricultrice** or **vigilatrice** are care workers with a year's training, often given by the local municipalities, but the number of staff with this qualification is declining. The qualification awards are not officially recognised and are unregulated. The diversity of courses affects quality but this area of training was not included in the review of the 1990s.

Combined centres

In the early 1970s responsibility for early childhood services was delegated to the regions from national control. Some local authorities, especially in the north, took the opportunity to build up their services for children under three years and in some cases developed innovatory provision.

In northern and central Italy some local authorities have developed **nuove tipologie**, also known as **servizi integrativi**. This provision offers combined care and educational centres with a range of services to children from birth to six years and their parents. Some are located in existing asili nidi but others are in separate buildings. The centres may support the day care needs of working parents but also aim to invite non-employed parents and other carers into the provision for social contact and support. There is also often an attempt to involve and make links with private local organisations.

REGGIO EMILIA

The best known example in the UK is probably the provision developed in the municipality of Reggio Emilia in northern Italy.

The approach evolved from the ideas of local parents and a teacher, Loris Malaguzzi (1920–94), who believed that the education of young children was a public task for the community at large and not just the private responsibility of individual families. Any community needs its children and the credo of the Reggio approach is that investment in children is a productive investment. The philosophy of the service also had its roots in a reaction to the fascist regime in Italy that fell with the end of the Second World War. There was strong local feeling that the community needed to raise children who were able to think for themselves and the Reggio Emilia early education system was founded on the perspective of the child.

Early attempts at numeracy

The provision in the region of Reggio Emilia includes centres for under threes and pre-primary schooling for three to six year olds. It is a useful example of how innovatory provision can be a source of cross-national learning. However, it must be remembered that this municipality is not typical of all Italy. About 40% of the local public spending has been devoted to early education, although economic recession has made this commitment less secure for the future.

Family day care

There is no organised or regulated system of family day care. Carers are self-employed and make private arrangement with families. Family day care is rare and private non-subsidised services are usually through a carer working in the child's own home.

Family obligations and employment

In 1996 Italy had an employment rate of 43% for mothers of under tens. However the national figure includes significant regional variations. The more prosperous north of the country has one of the highest maternal employment rates in the EU but rates are considerably lower in the south.

With some regional exceptions, day care is still generally viewed as a problem for mothers who choose to have jobs. Political awareness has grown of the issues of reconciling employment with family obligations but financial pressures reduce the will to develop any kind of coherent national response. Female employment is especially increasing in the service sector and accounts for two-thirds of women's employment in rural areas.

Italy offers a possible total of nine months combined maternity and parental leave, including care of sick children, not necessarily paid.

Early childhood education

The statutory school age in Italy is six years of age and from 1958 the national government took responsibility for developing early years education. Over twenty-five years a system was developed for three to six year olds that provided almost complete coverage of the age group. Since 1968 pre-primary education has been an official part of the state education system, although attendance is voluntary. This development moved the scuole materne, which were then pre-school educational facilities, out of the control of the Catholic Church and under the responsibility of the national Ministry of Education. About half of all the scuole materne are run by the state and the remainder are run by private organisations, usually religious.

The **scuole materne** provide pre-primary schooling from three years to school entry at six years of age. The settings are also known as a **scuole dell'infanzia**. Most children attend on a full-day basis, although the hours vary between regions. Attendance is free of charge in any state-run provision and also in the scuole materne run by local bodies. Transport is also provided for children when it is necessary, given the distances they may have to travel in rural and mountainous areas.

Ratios vary, but usually should be one teacher to 10 to 11 children. Classes can be one teacher with two assistants to a group of 25 to 28 children. Under legislation in 1992, disabled children are supposed to be integrated into the scuole materne with an appropriate reduction in the group size. A specialist teacher, **insegnante di sostegno,** is employed for a minimum of four disabled children.

Nearly all the scuole materne follow government guidelines for the curriculum, revised in 1991, that focus on meeting educational objectives within a rounded approach to development, including religious development. The Ministry of Education determines policy and training and the regional authorities implement national guidance with scope for local needs. The aims of the scuole materne are that the curriculum should support children's all-round development with the recognition that these are the citizens of the future. There is also a focus on preparing children for school. The national guidance stresses parental involvement but local implementation varies.

There are regional variations but overall a high percentage of three to six year olds (about 91% in 1991) attend a scuola materna. The levels vary between 97% in the northern provinces and 75% in the south and the islands of Sardinia and Sicily. The scuole materne run by the state, in contrast with private settings, have different forms of parent involvement and attendance at parents' evenings is obligatory.

TRAINING

The scuole materne are staffed by workers with a range of qualifications and some changes in training are planned.

Insegnanti di scuole materne (pre-primary teachers) had a three year course at tertiary level which is planned to be changed to a four year degree course. In the 1990s a five year broad vocational course led to the qualification of **assistenti di communita infantile** (social educators) but there is some discussion of raising the course to a university level. These workers can also be employed to work with adolescents and elderly people. **Assistenti per l'infanzia** are childcare assistants who had a three year course at a vocational school and they may also work in playschemes of different kinds. This assistant level was replaced in 1991 by the **operatore dei servizi sociali** (social care worker), who follows a three year course at a vocational school that also allows work with adolescents and elderly people. A **maestra elementare** (a primary school teacher) can also apply to work at the pre-primary level in a scuola materna.

Basic training is sometimes regarded as inadequate such that some northern regions have established patterns of continued training in post. Some regions have a **coordinatrice pedagogica** (early years coordinator) to develop training and service quality in all the local services of the asili nidi and scuole materne.

Statutory education

Primary schooling

Children start school at six years and can attend pre-primary from three years. Compulsory schooling lasts until children are thirteen years. School hours vary between the regions. The school day is usually longer in the north and schools in southern Italy sometimes finish by the early afternoon. The difference between school holidays and the average annual leave for employed adults is six and a half weeks.

Out-of-school provision

Services providing care and recreation for school age children are called **servizio extra-scolastico**. The limited available provision is sometimes on school premises but may be in leisure time centres and some summer holiday play schemes called **centro estivo**. The staff may have qualified as an **animatrice (**playworker) and have followed a course than can vary in length and is not officially recognised as a qualification. Out-of-school provision is mainly limited to the large towns and to the north and centre of the country. Provision is managed by the local authority. There is no national policy on out-of-school care and no reliable figures on the level of provision.

12

Luxembourg

National background

Geographical location

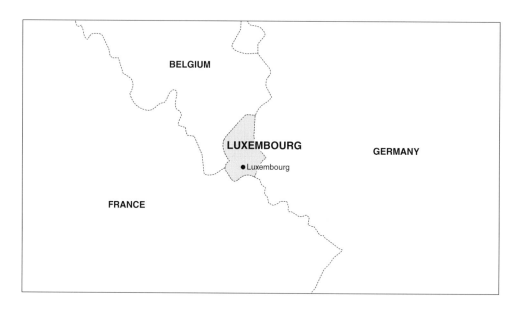

Luxembourg is the smallest country within the EU. It is, for instance, only twice the size of one of the north London boroughs (Islington) in the UK. Luxembourg has only land borders and is encircled by Belgium in the west and north, France in the south and Germany in the north–east and east.

Luxembourg's landscape is a mix of higher and lower plateau regions but none are more than about 500 metres high (under 1900 feet).

Politics and government

The Grand Duchy of Luxembourg is a constitutional monarchy with a parliamentary form of government. Executive power rests with the Grand

Duke, who appoints members to an advisory Council of State and to the Court of Justice. The Prime Minister and Chamber of Deputies are elected democratically by the population.

Social and economic framework

Luxembourg's central position in Europe has historically given the country an importance greater than its small size would imply. The country is too small to be self sustaining and Luxembourg's economy is striking for its close links with other European countries.

Luxembourg has industry and manufacturing, but has also developed as a significant financial and telecommunications centre, not only for Europe but also with countries in the rest of the world. The Luxembourg economy is prosperous, supported by its thriving financial sector. The country has a high standard of living, second only to the Swiss in Europe, and a comprehensive social welfare system.

Luxembourg has been of central significance in Europe and was a founding member of several international economic organisations. Luxembourg was one of the original group of six countries who formed in 1958 what became the EU.

LANGUAGE

There are three main language groups in the country:

- ▶ Letzeburgesch, for which the linguistic roots are German and French.
- ▶ Most of the population also speak standard French, which is used for most official purposes, and is the reason that all the terms in this chapter are given in French.
- ▶ German is also spoken as a daily language by some of the population.

POPULATION

Luxembourg has a population of 0.4 million, of whom 19% are under 15 years of age. The nation has a higher proportion of foreign-born people in the population than any other European country. Almost 30% of the population have migrated to Luxembourg from other countries of origin, mainly Portugal, Italy and other southern European countries. Migration was encouraged to meet the labour shortage arising from Luxembourg's very low birth rate.

URBAN-RURAL

Luxembourg has experienced steady migration from the more rural to the urban areas. Luxembourg City (the capital) in particular has attracted internal migrants to the jobs in the service and financial sectors. The population has become increasingly concentrated in the south-west of the country. Just under three-quarters of the country is classified as rural. However, since Luxembourg is a small country, no regions are far from a town.

Pre-school provision

Children start school at six years. However, in 1992 pre-primary education from four years became part of the official school system. Attendance become technically compulsory but is not a legal requirement until six years. The main aim of making the pre-primary provision compulsory was to offer minority ethnic groups, who comprise a third of the population, greater educational opportunity and to ease their integration into Luxembourg society as a whole.

The two systems of day care and early education are kept separate. The compulsory pre-primary schooling is the responsibility of the national Ministry of Education. Services for the under fours and out-of-school care is the responsibility of the Ministry of the Family.

Day care centres

Day care for the under fours is mainly run by private agencies, although supervised in a general way by the national Ministry of the Family. The provision is less regulated than the pre-primary schooling and consequently more diverse. Some private centres operate with very limited regulation. Parents pay fees that, in the state approved centres, can be related to family income.

The general name for day care centres is **foyers de jour.** The different kinds of centre may offer care for different age groups including school age children up to twelve years. **Crèches** tend to offer provision from birth to three years. The **centres d'enfants** cater for four to twelve year olds and, like the crèches, offer full-day all-year-round care. Priority is often given to lone parents, working parents and to families who experience social and economic disadvantage. **Garderies** offer short term sessional care for two to four year olds, either within a day care centre or on separate premises.

Since 1990 there has been an expansion of services for children under four years and especially for the under twos, with a view that they should be accessible to all families, as part of a coherent social policy. There has been particular concern to reach the more under-resourced regions in the northern part of Luxembourg. The approved centres increased their places by 39%. Availability of provision remains higher in the urban than the more rural areas and many rural families appear to cope through care by relatives in the family.

There have also been initiatives to provide **foyers de jour porte ouverte** (open door day care centres) and other provision for areas of social disadvantage. The open door centres usually cater for four to twelve year olds as a separate age group from the twelve to sixteen year olds. The aim of such expansion has also been to develop intercultural work and ease the integration of different ethnic groups into the society.

Reliable figures for the total provision are hard to obtain because over half the centres are privately run. Estimates are calculated from data derived from centres under government contract and who also receive a government subsidy. These government-funded and approved centres are called **foyers de jour conventionnés**. The **foyers de jour non-conventionnés** receive a government subsidy but are not subject to detailed approval. The approved centres have a ratio of one adult to five children who are not yet walking and then one adult to eight older children.

Between 1992 and 1993 the number of places in the approved centres increased by 49% for under twos, 19% for two to four year olds and 18% for over four year olds (in order to provide out-of-school provision). Waiting lists remain long for the centres. It is estimated that in all the foyers de jour there are about 5.4% of one year olds, 7.8% of one to two year olds, 15% of two to three year olds and 19.2% of three to four year olds.

WORKFORCE

The foyers de jour are usually staffed by **éducateurs gradué** (social educators) who have followed a broad based three year course at a higher education institute and are also qualified to work with other age groups of children and adolescents and in a range of social care roles.

Staff may still hold the lower qualification of **éducateur**. This qualification originally focussed on remedial work and with disabled children. The changes in training of the 1990s have broadened the scope of the courses, hence newly trained workers are called éducateur gradué. However, the course content still covers disabled children.

The centre groups with children under eighteen months may also have an **infirmière en pédiatrie** (children's nurse). The programme for children can vary although it is usually more focussed on play and child-initiated activities than the curriculum of the jardins d'enfants.

Family day care

Called **assistant maternelle** or **Tagesmutter**, family day care is a limited form of provision and unregulated. Reliable statistics are hard to obtain, estimated figures are for about 4% of children under seven years.

Since 1990 there has been some development of family day care to meet the needs of disabled children who are placed with a carer by social workers. Carers are limited to three children at one time.

Family obligations and employment

Compared with many other EU countries, Luxembourg has a relatively low percentage of employed mothers with children under ten years. 42% of this group are in employment, with 29% of then in part-time jobs. There is no clear relationship between levels of maternal employment and age of children in the family. Despite the efforts to develop provision there is still a gap in terms of day care needs.

Early childhood education

In the 1960s there was significant expansion in early years education and the terms **éducation (or enseignement) préscolaire** (pre-school education) and **jardin d'enfants** (nursery school) became part of national legislation.

Pre-primary education is jointly the responsibility of the national Ministry of Education and the local authorities. All municipalities were required to set up jardins d'enfants and the state has established regulations for training. The pre-primary schooling centre is called a **jardin d'enfants** in the French language community, **spillschoul** in Letzeburgisch and **Kindergärten** or **Vorschule** in the German. These settings are usually attached to a primary school and follow the same hours and terms.

The national legislative framework determines much of the detail of the curriculum, methods and organisation of the jardins d'enfants. The objective is that children are prepared socially and cognitively for school learning. The local authorities deal with buildings and equipment. Neither pre-primary nor primary settings tend to have heads in charge of the school and teachers are directly answerable to the inspectors. Settings often have a Parents' Association but the role is purely consultative and parents have limited influence on the running of a school.

Attendance at a jardin d'enfants is compulsory and free of charge to parents. Non-attendance is not an offence under the law, as it becomes after the age of six years, but close to 100% of the age range does attend. Families are told which jardin d'enfants their child will attend and authorities in rural areas organise transport where necessary.

The programme for four to six year olds includes graded learning objectives within a rounded approach to child development. The aim is partly that of preparation for school, but the curriculum is also shaped by the ideas of Froebel and Montessori. There is an increased awareness of multilingual families, most of whom are from Portugal and Italy. Specific encouragement is given to learning Letzeburgesch, to support the ability of children from other countries of origin to be able to join in the whole life of the school. In some regions over half the children in a pre-primary or primary class can be from a foreign country of origin.

The jardins d'enfants are staffed by an **instituteur de l'éducation préscolaire** (pre-school teacher) trained for three years at a Higher Education Institute linked with a university. The training enables people to specialise in work with four to six year olds. The teacher is often supported by an assistant. The Ministry of Education recommends a ratio of one teacher to 14–18 children, but local authorities do not always follow the guidance.

The aim is that disabled children should be integrated into mainstream services but this is a recent development. Through the 1990s there has been some focus to ensure that all state-run centres can offer a quality service to disabled children. Funds for extra staff and allowing families to avoid any waiting lists are further measures of support.

Statutory education

Primary schooling

Children start school at six years of age and compulsory education lasts for nine years until children are fifteen.

Some form of provision is important for working parents despite the high attendance at pre-primary. The hours of the jardins d'enfants do not cover the mid-day break and they are closed on some afternoons. Primary schools have three full and three half days and children are usually expected to go home for the two hour mid-day break. Some employers allow parents an extended lunchtime to deal with this period of the day. However, the time has to be made up at the beginning or end of the working day, so simply moves the problem elsewhere. The difference between the school holidays and average annual leave for employed adults is ten and a half weeks.

Out-of-school provision

Some children attend the foyers de jour to cover the out-of-school hours of an adult working day and as a consequence often make several trips to and fro during a single day. In 1993 about 3% of four to ten year olds were attending a foyer de jour in addition to school. A minority of local authorities have **foyers de midi**, provision that offers children a mid-day meal and care beyond school hours.

A range of measures were being discussed through the 1990s in terms of more flexible working hours for parents and opening hours in centres. Such out-of-school care that is available may be run by private organisations, local authorities or employers. The staff tend to be qualified as an éducateur gradué or éducateur.

13

The Netherlands

National background

Geographical location

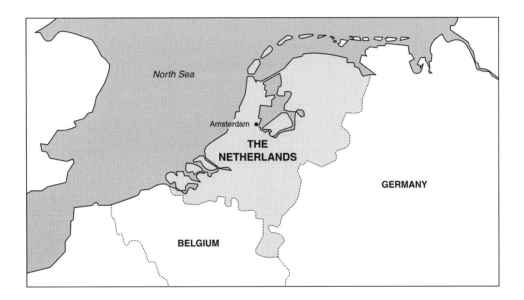

The Netherlands is located in north-western Europe. It has a coastal boundary in the north and west with the North Sea and land borders with Germany in the east and Belgium in the south. Almost 20% of the country comprises inland water areas. The country has also been known to outsiders as Holland, but strictly that description only applies to the two western coastal provinces, called south and north Holland. The country has a temperate maritime climate and this pattern does not vary much between the regions.

The name of The Netherlands ('nether' in Dutch means low) relates to the fact that it is a predominantly low-lying country, the highest point of which is 321 metres. In the south and east are natural lowlands and plains, whereas the coastal areas of the north and west are almost all below sea level. About one-quarter of the country lies below sea level, the lowest point, near Rotterdam, is 6.7 metres below sea level.

This situation has resulted from a process of land drainage and reclamation from the North Sea lasting for centuries, although the biggest projects were undertaken during the twentieth century. In total about one-fifth of the country is land reclaimed from the sea and the river estuaries. As a consequence continual drainage, with storm and flood control from the North Sea and the rivers, are a major national concern.

Politics and government

The Kingdom of The Netherlands is one of the EU countries with a monarchy still in place. The royal family has a limited constitutional role, much as in the UK, and the country is governed by an elected parliament. The Netherlands also includes the self-governing island of Aruba and the former colony of the Antilles.

Social and economic framework

The Netherlands was one of the original group of six countries who in 1958 formed what became the EU.

The country is heavily agricultural, with three-fifths of the land, including the reclaimed areas (the polders), used for dairy animal pasture, farms and market gardens, including the growing of flowers. However, the agricultural part of the economy accounts for less than 5% of the gross national product (GNP). Financial services and industry are important. The GNP is growing faster than the population and The Netherlands enjoys a prosperous standard of living similar to that of other developed EU countries.

Many aspects of society were traditionally organised along religious lines so that trade unions, political parties and schools belonged to one of the four major groupings of Catholic, Protestant, Socialist and Liberal. Dutch society has become increasingly secular, although the divisions can still be seen in the educational structure.

LANGUAGE

Most of the population speak Netherlandic (Dutch), a language shared with the Flemish community in Belgium and an area in north-west France where a Dutch dialect is spoken. Frisian is the second language of residents of Friesland in the north-east of the country.

POPULATION

In 1998 the population was 15.7 million, of whom 18% were under fifteen years of age. The country is one of the most densely populated in the world. In 1993 the fertility rate was 1.57.

Foreign-born residents include immigrants from Turkey, Morocco, the UK and the former Dutch colony of Surinam. A proportion of the foreign workers return to their country of origin.

URBAN-RURAL

Although the overall population density is high in The Netherlands, two-fifths of the total live in three provinces to the west-central part of the country, that includes the cities of Amsterdam (the capital), Rotterdam, The Hague and Utrecht. In the north-eastern provinces the population density is markedly lower. Urban areas account for more than 88% of the population of The Netherlands.

Pre-school provision

The Netherlands has a split system of educational provision for four to six year olds and day care within welfare for the under fours. Compulsory schooling starts at age five years, but almost all (about 95%) four year olds are in school.

Day care centres

Day care of children is privately organised and the responsibility of the Ministry of Health, Welfare and Sport at national level and local authorities in the regions. The focus of day care is generally seen to be a service for working parents, with a secondary objective of promotion of children's development. There is a continuing debate about the balance of care and learning in the day care settings, and whether they can be educational.

There was a government initiative scheme (The Stimulative Measure on Childcare) during 1990–5 to support the expansion of childcare provision, both for younger children and for out-of-school care. This initiative has considered a variety of services with the outlook that about 70% of places should be funded by parents and employers, leaving a minority, about 30%, to be funded jointly by local authorities and parents.

The development of day care services is viewed almost exclusively as a response to maternal employment. Services are expected to be market driven and vary according to the local needs arising from employment, which can create discontinuities in provision. Generally the state meets about one-third of the childcare costs and the rest is met by parents' fees and employers.

The attempt to expand day care provision has been within a framework of increased decentralisation and deregulation of the provision. In this atmosphere of increasing privatisation and market driven services, minimum quality standards were introduced for the second half of the 1990s on a five year experimental period. Early years specialists in The Netherlands have been concerned to raise the issue of quality and needs of children. Professionals wish to counter-balance the political focus on quantity, the needs of the market place and on those parents who are in the kind of employment where they can meet the costs.

There are a number of different kinds of day care centres, all of which are more common in urban than rural areas.

- ▶ The **kinderdagverblijven** developed as a provision for working mothers and until the expansion of the first half of the 1990s were available in very low numbers. These centres usually work on a full-day and all-year-round basis and take children from two months to four years. Some centres also offer out-of-school care up to about thirteen years.
- ▶ Some centres are open the year round but for a shorter day, about five hours, and these are called a **halvedagverblijf**.
- ▶ When centres are workplace nurseries they are called a **bedrijfscrèche** and very few of these centres provide for school age children.
- ▶ **Oudercrèches** are centres managed by parents, who may work alongside the paid staff.
- ▶ **The particuliere crèche** is run by a small private company and the **crèche aan huis** by a carer in her own home.

The centres run on a full-day basis but the younger children can be offered shorter hours.

In 1993 about 12% of under fours attended the different centres and were mostly the children of working mothers or students. The European Commission Network on Childcare estimated that about 8% of under threes had places. Since some children do not attend full-time the number of children exceeds the number of places and the figures are estimates.

In 1987 responsibility for the funding and management of day care was delegated to the local authorities and only a few matters of regulations are still central. There are no national regulations about ratios but the Association of Dutch Municipalities recommends 2:8 for children under a year, 2:10 for one to two years, 2:12 for two to three years and 2:16 for three to four years of age. All staff should have a qualification or be in training.

WORKFORCE

The staff in this sector have a broad based training, which may not focus much on childcare, or a two year on site training. There are a number of different vocational training courses and the diversity is a matter of some concern in The Netherlands, if quality is to be an issue in day care.

Staff may be a **leidster kinder centra** (care worker) with two years training of an apprenticeship nature within the day care centre. Additional training is required to become a head of centre, **hoofd**, with four years training and possibly an additional one year on management.

Training as a leidster is the only pattern that focusses on working with children in a day care setting. Other staff in a centre may have a general vocational training background gained at senior secondary level leading to a number of different role titles and the possibility of working in many social care settings besides childcare. Since 1984 there have no longer been any training courses that focus specifically on early childhood education and care.

Family day care

This form of provision is known as **gastouderopvang** (literally care in guest families) and is controlled by the Ministry of Social Affairs although families make individual agreements with the carers. The individual **gastouder** may work with a **gastouderbureau**, a local office which organises, but does not employ the carers, brings families together with carers and offers advice and training. In 1994 about 1.3% of under fours were in this kind of provision. There are no national requirements but it is recommended that family day carers have no more than four children, including their own.

Family obligations and employment

The Netherlands has a low number of working mothers in comparison with many other EU countries and many work part-time. In 1991 40% of mothers with a child under ten years were employed and this was a 17% rise since 1985. In 1993 49% of mothers with children under ten years were in jobs and only 12% of them were in full-time employment, the lowest proportion in EU countries. The Netherlands offers a total of fifteen months of combined maternity and parental leave (part-time and not full-time), not necessarily paid. There is no leave to care for sick children.

It seems that employment levels may be higher in some of the rural peri-urban areas than in the fully urban regions, with employment predominantly in the service industries. Day care provision is very limited in rural areas and many families seem to manage through care within their own family or family day care.

Childcare has long been regarded as a private matter for families to handle or in cooperation with employers, rather than a matter for state involvement. In this outlook, The Netherlands shares perspectives with the UK, Ireland and Germany. But, like those EU countries, The Netherlands has begun to consider the alternative perspective in the last couple of decades of the twentieth century. The pressure towards more effective childcare was driven partly as a result of wanting more women in the labour market and as an issue in gender equality.

Playgroups

The Netherlands has a playgroup movement developed during the 1960s. The **peuterspeelzalen** are set up as parents' cooperatives for two and three year old children and were attended by slightly over half that age group in 1993. A peuterspeelzaal offers sessional places and children do not necessarily attend each day of the week, so the number of children attending the peuterspeelzalen is more than twice the number of places. Parents pay fees, which are usually fixed, and only a minority of groups relate fees to family income.

The playgroup movement had similar concerns to other national movements about children's learning through play and to a certain extent preparation for school. However in 1987 the peuterspeelzalen came under the responsibility of local authorities and have had to fulfil similar requirements to the day care centres on size. Peuterspeelzalen are sometimes used as a placement for children from socially disadvantaged families or for children from minority ethnic groups.

One or two workers must be professionally trained to the intermediate vocational level. The qualified **peuterspeelzaalleidster** may have a two or three year training course, but may also have learned on the job.

Early childhood education

Pre-school educational facilities developed during the nineteenth and twentieth century and were initially based on the ideas of Pestalozzi and Froebel, and later on Montessori. After the Second World War the **kleuterscholen** (nursery schools) became a widespread and free provision for four and five year olds. Then in 1985 the pre-school educational stage was fully integrated into the compulsory system of primary schooling to form **basisonderwijs** (basic education) for four to twelve year olds. Within the same change, the training of kindergarten educators was merged with that of primary school teachers. The whole system is the responsibility of the Ministry of Education, Science and the Arts.

Children can attend the **basisschool** from four years and the schools are either state-run or run by private agencies, in most cases church organisations (Catholic, Protestant or other denominations). The vast majority of four year olds attend school. In 1992 the figures were 98% for boys and 99% for girls.

The settings are run by a **leerkracht basisschool**, who is a teacher, trained for four years at a tertiary college to work with children from four to twelve years of age.

There is a long-running debate in The Netherlands about an appropriate model for education in the basisschool for the four to six year olds and the slightly older range of six to eight year olds. The integration of pre-schooling into the compulsory system raised its status, but created concerns that some of the younger children attended inappropriately large groups and that the curriculum often lost the emphasis on learning through play and attention to individual needs. The related concern is that the combined training gives insufficient time to the younger age range. It is now possible to follow the first three years of teacher training with a one year specialisation in either four to eight year olds or eight to twelve year olds.

Statutory education

Primary schooling

Children can start school at four years and most do. However, education is compulsory full-time from five to sixteen years, and part-time up to eighteen years. Schooling is free to parents, although some schools ask for a contribution.

The 'normal' look of provision for children has changed over the second half of the twentieth century

Schools include both state run and grant-aided private schools. The majority of children attend private schools that form about 75% of the total provision. The Constitution allows any group of people to establish a school on the basis of religious or philosophical belief or educational philosophy. Under the 1985 legislation, the national Ministry of Education determines the curriculum subjects and standards for all schools. Schools then draw up specific plans within this framework, including religious education in the denominational schools.

Schools usually run a full day except for half day on Wednesday. School hours increase slightly as children get older. Maternal employment is low in The Netherlands and the rate increases when a family's youngest child goes to school. The difference between the school holidays and the average annual leave for employed adults is 7 weeks.

Out-of-school provision

Since 1985, parents were given the right to organise supervision in the mid-day break, for which they pay or supervise unpaid themselves. The coverage of the lunchbreak is called **tussen-de-middag-opvang** and some schools organise their own supervision. Prior to this change, all children had to go home for lunch.

There is limited out-of-school provision, although services increased as part of the 1990s Stimulative Measure. Care in separate premises is called a **centrum voor buitenschoolse opvang**. The **kinderdagverblijven** offer school age care as well day care for the under fours. The out-of-school programme is generally within a relaxed atmosphere with choice of play activities. Some inner city schools offer an extended day, **velengde schooldag**.

Out-of-school care is publicly funded but run by private organisations. The recommendation is that there should be a ratio of two adults to eighteen children, who might be as young as four years. In 1993 about 1% of four to thirteen year olds were in out-of-school provision and 5% of ten to twelve year olds. The number of places had increased over fourfold since 1989. There is no specific qualification for working in out-of-school provision and staff may have any of the qualifications that are common in day care or pre-primary schooling. The ratio is usually recommended as two qualified adults for every 19 to 20 children.

14

Portugal

National background

Geographical location

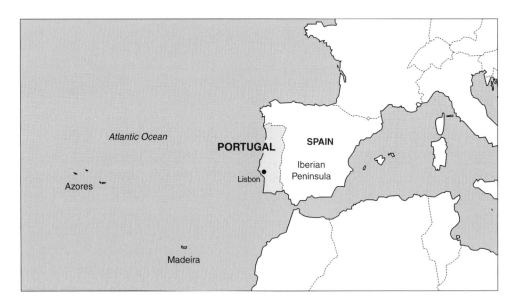

Portugal lies along the Atlantic coast of the Iberian Peninsula in south-western Europe and at the extreme western rim of the European continental mass. Portugal has a land border with Spain in the north and east and Portugal itself occupies only 16% of the Peninsula. The Atlantic islands of Madeira and the Azores are also a political and administrative part of Portugal. Macao in the Far East is only part of the former Portuguese colonial empire to remain a dependency.

Although Portugal has mountain ranges, the highest point in the country is 1993 metres (6539 feet) and less than 12% of the country lies above 700 metres (2300 feet). Coastal and southern lowlands create an otherwise relatively low-lying landscape.

Politics and government

Portugal is now a republic with a parliamentary form of government. However, it was run as an authoritarian dictatorship under President Salazar from the late 1920s until the 1974 revolution. There was some move towards greater democracy during the 1970s and then, in 1974, Salazar was removed from office. A new Constitution was established in 1976 and Portugal has since experienced a diversity of political parties and coalition governments tend to predominate. Full civilian rule was established in 1982.

Social and economic framework

Portugal experienced a later onset of industrialisation in comparison with many other central and northern EU countries. Portugal joined the EU in 1986 and was initially the poorest and least developed of EU countries. The country's position has improved somewhat although the economy is still rather vulnerable.

During the 1960s there was a significant exodus of men from rural areas as they sought work in the urban areas and migrated to other countries. Large numbers were involved in fighting during the wars of Portuguese colonies precipitated by Salazar's foreign policy. The colonial wars also led to the migration to Portugal of Portuguese from the former colonies, especially from Angola, and a high urban unemployment rate still persists.

The losses in the colonial wars, as well as illegal emigration to avoid conscription, added to the long term population imbalance, with women significantly outnumbering men. Hazardous male occupations including fishing, and also the legal emigration, contributed to the imbalance. The whole situation led to a noticeable increase in lone and employed mothers with a consequent pressure on childcare provision. Such measures were initially seen by the government as the responsibility of voluntary organisations but, after the 1974 revolution, childcare came to be seen more in connection with women's rights.

Language

The population of both the mainland and the islands speak Portuguese, which is one of the Romance languages in origin.

Population

In 1998 Portugal had a population of 10 million, of whom 17% were under fifteen years of age. The country has one of the higher fertility rates in Europe (1.52 in 1993) but also has a relatively high infant mortality rate.

Mainland Portugal is a mix of highlands, plateau regions and coastal lowlands. The country is largely rural, about 70% being classified as rural. The population is distributed unevenly between the more densely populated northern part of the country and the less populated south. There has been a movement of population from many of the rural areas to the more urban and some of the coastal areas, like the Algarve, and the central plains are now overpopulated for what the local economy can support.

Pre-school provision

A history of discontinuity and disruption

In Portugal early childhood education developed from the end of the nineteenth century with **jardim de infância** (nursery school) following the ideas of Froebel. A specifically Portuguese tradition developed from the ideas of João de Deus (see page 28). In the first four decades of the twentieth century early childhood education was in theory a political priority. However, extreme political instability, including 46 governments over one period of 16 years, meant that theory did not become reality.

The Salazar dictatorship gave no priority to pre-school education and removed the relevant responsibilities from the Ministry of Education. From the 1930s early years education was merged with a social welfare function and the educational perspective did not re-emerge until the 1950s and 60s. Increasing maternal employment was met by a diversity of measures under a number of other ministries. After the return to democratic government during the 1970s there was a rapid expansion in early childhood services, including an official recognition of early educational input. However, the diversity created in the middle of the twentieth century remains a significant feature of the systems of early years provision in Portugal.

In the first half of the 1970s the democratically elected government once more made pre-school education a state responsibility and part of the official education system. Jardims de infância were established by the Ministry of Education again from the late 1970s. A wide range of childcare and early educational provision grew at the local level but often with inadequate funding so that quality was a central issue. Forms of centralised state support and planning became more important and local initiatives ran out of funding or enthusiasm.

The expansion of pre-school education is now a very high government priority. However, debates continue about how both day care and pre-school education can be extended and quality also be maintained. One of the areas of disagreement is the balance between central government intervention and regulation, local autonomy and the extent to which privatisation can meet the needs of families.

The publicly funded services for children under six years, compulsory school age, operate as two systems for day care of the under sixes and the pre-school education of three to six year olds. The childcare settings may work to integrate an educational component into the children's day. However, the exclusively educational settings for over threes specifically do not try to address any day care needs for families.

Day care centres

The childcare system is separate from that for early education and national responsibility is held by the Ministry of Solidarity (covering employment and social security). However, provision is run by different bodies, some public, some private and some operating as cooperative organisations.

Private but non-profit-making associations have been important in establishing various types of day care provision in Portugal. One key player has been the IPSS, the Institucão Particular de Solidaridade Social (social solidarity private organisations). The IPSS facilities have a special status based on the contracts between the IPSS and the Ministry of Employment and Social Affairs. During the 1990s the IPSSs became increasingly important as service providers. Some additional provision is managed by local authorities and the Regional Social Security Centres.

As a consequence of past history, non-statutory childcare and educational provision varies considerably between regions of Portugal with differences in the details of the contracts setting up the provision, any regulations, the content of programmes for the children and the overall quality of provision. Parents pay fees that are usually related to family income.

Settings for children under three years are called a **crèche** or **infantário**. These settings offer full-day, all-year-round provision. Within the welfare system settings called **jardim de infância** offer full-day and all-year-round childcare for three to six year olds and may also offer a service to school age children. The **centro infantil** is an age integrated care setting which may offer provision from birth up to and including school age children. The ratios in the centres tend to be one adult to five or six children who are not yet walking, 1:8–10 for under threes, 2:15 three year olds and 2:25 three to six year olds.

The day care provision is generally oriented towards family needs, hours appropriate for working mothers and family support where necessary. There is an educational strand but within a broader family and social care approach. However, there is so much diversity within provision that any generalisations are difficult.

In 1993 there were day care places for about 12% of the under threes population. About 90% of the places were in crèches and the rest in family day care (see below). There was an expansion of provision from 1988 to 1993 when places in crèches increased by 25% and those in family day care by 130%. In 1993 an estimated 26% of three to six year olds had places in the jardims de infância within the welfare system and from 1988 to 1993 this provision increased by 15%.

Workforce

The staff of the crèches may be an **educador de infância** whose training is in a higher education institution for three years, although there is some discussion about changing the training to a four year university level course. Day care settings may also have staff with a more medical training such as an **enfermeira**, a nurse who has completed three years training at a tertiary level college. The centres tend to prefer nurses with a social care qualification, **enfermeira social**. The qualified staff are also supported by unqualified assistants, **pessoal auxiliar do técnico** who have varied training backgrounds. Large centres that combine the educational and care strands tend to be managed by a professional with a social work qualification, an **assistente sociale**, who has completed five years training at a university level institute.

Family day care

State regulated and funded family day care exists alongside unregulated private family day care. The **crèche familiar** is a pattern of coordinated family day care, usually for the under threes but sometimes for older children. Family day carers can take up to four children per person, or three if a child is disabled.

The system of crèche familiar is that groups of up to 20 **amas** (family day carers) are trained, licensed and managed by a local organising body which is also responsible for the allocation of children, payment, further training and monitoring the children's progress. The group is usually supervised by an educador de infância and sometimes by a qualified nurse. Between 12 to 20 family day carers are supervised by the advisory worker. There are no reliable figures on the numbers involved and the system is the overall responsibility of the Ministry of Solidarity (social welfare system) and the local authorities.

Family obligations and employment

Portugal has a high level of employment of mothers compared with many EU countries but a relatively low rate of provision of day care and early education. In 1996 70% of mothers of under tens were working (63% of them in full-time jobs). In 1993 70% of mothers of children under fifteen years were employed and 90% of them worked full-time, the highest rate of full-time working by mothers in the EU. The differences between the two figures also suggest that full-time working may increase slightly with the age of children.

Portugal offers a total of 27 months of maternity plus parental leave after the birth of each child, not necessarily paid. There is a low take up rate on the unpaid parental leave. Parents can take up to thirty days leave, only sometimes paid, per year to care for a sick child under ten years.

However the availability of day care is variable, with significant regional variations. There is often limited childcare in rural areas and most centres are offering pre-school education following school and not adult working hours. However, this is not just a rural shortage; some of the densely populated industrial areas have the lowest levels of provision. The cost of urban housing has also meant that some parents have long commuting journeys.

Early childhood education

The law for pre-school education 1996 defined this stage as the first part of the educational system. The curriculum generally aims to promote positive attitudes to learning for children, support all-round development, to offer support for problems and to ensure parents' involvement in the educational process.

▶ An educational model influenced by Freinet and Helen Keller places emphasis on cooperative and project-based activities and encouraging

children to take some responsibility for younger ones. Children are encouraged to be self-directed and there are few whole class activities.
▶ However, the settings influenced by João de Deus have a more adult-directed approach and a planned curriculum. The main goals remain fostering literacy and building the foundations for children to read.
▶ Another strand can be that of using education as a vehicle for social compensation. Following the 1974 revolution pre-school education and care has sometimes been given a role of supporting children and families at risk.

Pre-school educational provision for three to six year olds is offered in the **jardims de infância de rede pública.** The settings are open for similar hours and terms to the primary schools. The centres are free to parents and attendance is voluntary. In 1993 about 22% of this age group attended jardims within the educational system and provision has fallen slightly (by 1%) since 1988.

Children in the jardims may be in mixed age groupings or same age and the size of the groups varies considerably between centres. The staff are usually a qualified educador de infancia supported by an unqualified assistant, **auxiliar educativo**. The ratios are one and a half adults to every fifteen three year olds or to twenty-five three to six year olds.

There are some sessional pre-school services in rural areas that mainly serve five year olds but no reliable figures are available. The provision is called **educaçao dê infancia itinerante** and are mobile services designed to reach families in the more remote areas with few or no centres. During the 1990s the government also launched some experimental programmes of early education to reach children in urban disadvantaged areas of Lisbon (the capital) and Porto.

TRANSITION INTO COMPULSORY SCHOOL

A discussion continues in Portugal, as in most other EU countries, about how best to support children as they make the move into statutory school at six years of age. One aspect is the education of the large numbers of children from minority ethnic families, many of whom have migrated from former Portuguese colonies. The children sometimes experience learning or adjustment difficulties within the school system.

Statutory education

Primary schooling

Children attend school from six years to fourteen on a compulsory basis. Primary schooling is free to parents. Schools tend to shut by mid-afternoon and do not usually provide food or supervision over the lunchbreak. The difference between school holidays and the average annual leave for employed adults is eleven and a half weeks.

Out-of-school provision

Actividades de tempos livres is the general term covering any care or recreation facilities for school age children. The centres are called **centro de actividades de tempos livres** (CATLs) and often share premises with services for younger children in a centro infantil. Parents contribute to the costs of out-of-school provision. In 1993 there were places for about 10% of the six to ten year age group in CATLs but not all the places were filled. There was an increase in level of provision of 45% between 1988 and 1993.

Hours and conditions vary and the settings come under the national responsibility of the Ministry of Solidarity, within the social welfare system, and are financed locally by the regional authority or parents' associations. There is a specific aim of providing services in areas of high maternal employment and of social disadvantage.

The particular forms of provision are often organised by voluntary associations attached to IPSS who run day care for under sixes. The provision is diverse, including some holiday playschemes, homework clubs and projects with the explicit aim to intervene with families at risk. Ratios tend to be two adults to twenty children and the focus is on freely chosen activities and helping children to discover new interests. Larger centres used to have a more formal educational and homework focus but the play orientation seems to be widespread now.

In centres the children are often with a qualified educador de infância or a teacher. Some assistants have specifically trained in leisure time provision and are called **animador cultural** or **animador social**. The three year training takes place in the vocational branch of the upper secondary school but the qualification has not gained an official recognition.

15

Spain

National background

Geographical location

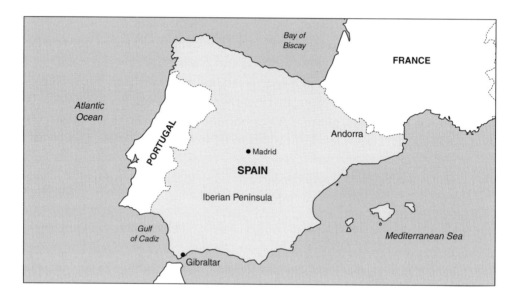

Spain is one of Europe's largest countries and is located in the south-west corner of the continent on the Iberian Peninsula. The country's land borders include France and Andorra to the north-east and Portugal in the west, with whom Spain shares the Peninsula. In the most southerly part of the country there is a border with Gibraltar, a small enclave run by the UK and a continuing source of political friction. In the east and south-east the country has a coastal border with the Mediterranean Sea and in the west with the Atlantic Ocean through the Gulf of Cadiz in the south-west and the Bay of Biscay in the north.

Spain also includes the Balearic Islands, the largest of which is Majorca, which lie to the east of the mainland in the Mediterranean Sea and the

Canary Islands to the south west in the Atlantic Ocean. Spain also retains control of two cities in northern Morocco in north Africa.

Although UK visitors to Spain are more likely to know the coastal regions, the country as a whole is dominated by the Meseta, a large central plateau surrounded by mountain ranges. The highest point is 3478 metres (11 411 feet) in the Sierra Nevada in the south.

Politics and government

Spain is one of Europe's oldest nation states. It now has a constitutional monarchy and is officially the Kingdom of Spain.

Following the Spanish civil war in the mid-1930s the country experienced several decades of an authoritarian fascist regime under President Franco. The dictatorship established in 1939 ended with Franco's death in 1975 and the subsequent social and political changes led to a democratic political system. In 1969 Franco had designated the head of the Spanish royal family as his successor. Juan Carlos restored the monarchy in 1975 and led the country into a democratic system. The monarch is the official head of state but the government is run by the elected parliament, all of which was established within the 1978 Constitution.

Spain had traditionally been relatively isolated from the rest of Europe, but the election of a democratic government led to closer links and in 1986 Spain joined the EU.

From a very centralised system of government, a long process of decentralisation was begun, which is still continuing. Spain has seventeen autonomous regional communities called comunidades autónomas, six of which have full responsibility for the local education services.

Social and economic framework

Spain has a developed market economy and the government has fostered the development of heavy industries. The Spanish economy is also based on services, manufacturing, agriculture and tourism, especially on the eastern coastal regions and the islands. The economy is buoyant and the gross national product (GNP) is one of the highest in Europe.

LANGUAGE

The main language of Spain is Castilian Spanish, although Catalan Spanish (a rather different version of the language), Galician, Valencian and the Basque language are also spoken by large communities and co-exist as official languages within those regions. The Basque community in north of Spain has a long-standing independence movement.

POPULATION

In 1998 the country had a population of 39.4 million, of whom 19% were under fifteen years of age. The fertility rate was 1.26 in 1993.

URBAN-RURAL

The Spanish population mainly lives in towns and cities, more than three-quarters of the population are urban. Despite building programmes, there is an urban housing shortage. The rural areas are varied and while some have a declining population others are experiencing a population increase and local development.

Pre-school provision

The move towards an integrated system

There was an expansion of early childhood provision in the 1960s, especially in terms of state-run centres for three to six year olds. Reforms introduced in the 1970s established a pre-school educational stage prior to the eight years of compulsory schooling. A second wave of change followed in the 1990s.

Previously day care and education were divided into two separate systems with their own organisation and training. In 1990 an Education Reform Act, the Ley de Ordenacion General del Sistema Educativo (LOGSE) established a new framework to the early years with the concept of early childhood education extending from birth to the statutory school age of six years.

This development is innovatory for any of the EU countries, especially since the integrated system is located within the educational system and not welfare. The whole system is the responsibility of the national Ministry of Education and the education departments of the regional communities with control over this area of public provision. The management of publicly funded early childhood services can be delegated to local authority organisations or private agencies that sign an agreement with the education authorities. There has been a tendency to delegate the social services to private agencies.

The period of **educación infantil** (early childhood education) is divided
into two cycles – birth to three years and three to six years – but the goals
for each cycle are very similar and stress a holistic approach to children's all-
round development. The objective was to bring centres for the under threes
into the educational framework and to end the traditional care-education
divide.

Whatever the age of the children, the aim is that staff should be qualified
early childhood teachers, with a three year university level training. The
very earliest years are viewed as an educational as well as a care situation and
not just as a service for children in need. The curriculum policy supports a
view that the birth to six years period is an educational and contextualisation
stage. It is striking that this development was not driven from economic
needs, since Spain has a relatively low level of maternal employment
compared with other European countries.

Although Spain was the first European country to adopt a national policy of
early childhood education from birth, the implementation of the policy is far
from complete. Financial constraints including staffing have limited full
development of the policy into actual practice. The economic recession that

Celebrating a birthday

Spain has experienced with much of the rest of the EU has slowed the intended programme of change. The government gave priority to ensuring places for the three to six year olds and less focus on provision for the younger children.

A further problem lies within the Spanish early years profession itself, which has tended to see pre-school education as having a major goal of preparation for school. This outlook arises from the history of the pre-school tradition in Spain that developed as an extension of statutory schooling rather than as a separate tradition. In contrast with other EU countries who had a strong pre-school service with its own character, Spanish pre-school professionals have predominantly seen the years before statutory schooling as a time to support school readiness, especially if children came from socially disadvantaged family backgrounds. Such an objective does not relate well to a more holistic approach that can appropriately incorporate the very youngest children.

A system in transition

Despite the political commitment following the 1990 Act there are still different systems for day care and educational services in the period before children start school at six years of age. Spain also has considerable regional variation. The 1990 reform introduced different terminology but inevitably there are some inconsistencies and potential confusion. The objective is to move towards national standards for the curriculum, staff qualifications and ratios and minimum requirements within any setting. The programme for children also includes learning the relevant local language in those communities where Castilian Spanish is not the only home language.

NEW CENTRES

There are three kinds of setting that offer pre-school provision as envisaged by the 1990 LOGSE:

▶ The **escuelas infantiles** may be first or second stage schools for children up to three years, or for those from three to six years. These settings are the responsibility of the local authorities or autonomous communities that do not have responsibility for education. The name of a setting may specify the age range, for instance, escuela infantil 0–3.
▶ The **escuelas de educación infantil** are the second stage schools for children from three to six years. These settings are the responsibility of the Ministry of Education or those autonomous communities that have a responsibility for education.

▶ Integrated age centres, **centros de educación infantil,** are open to children across the whole age range up to six years. These may be private or public provision. They may be called escuela infantil 0–6.

The hours of the new style centres are not uniform but they tend to be more flexible and longer than the old style centres (see page 166) which follow primary school hours. Some settings offer full-day and all-year-round service.

The required ratios tend to be 1:7 for children under a year old, 1:10 for toddlers from one to two years, 1:18 for two to three year olds and 1:25 for three to six year olds (but can be 1:30 in private settings). Some regions require more favourable ratios for their local settings.

The cost to parents can vary. In publicly funded settings, they will probably pay some contribution to costs for the earlier stage (under threes) although the second stage will probably be free. Private settings will charge fees.

The aim is that the new early childhood centres will be staffed by two new types of professional:

▶ **maestro especialista en educación infantil** (early childhood education teacher) who will have three years training at university level;
▶ **técnico superior (**or **especialista) en educación infantil** (senior early childhood worker) also called **educador infantil** who will have a training at the higher vocational educational level of about a year. These workers can be responsible for under threes and work as an assistant to a maestro for over threes.

There are transition arrangements up to the year 2000 to enable the changes to be organised. The programme for the centres has to develop from the more structured, school preparation orientation of the previous kindergarten tradition. However, the evidence from Spain suggests that the pace of reform has been slow and the previous pattern of centres, now described, still applies in many places.

Day care settings

Private agencies usually run settings more focussed on care, mainly for the under threes and offering full-day cover. The word **guardería** generally covers care settings. The guarderías are usually privately run and pre-1990 were rarely inspected on an official basis. The custodial approach rather than a more explicitly educational orientation still tends to dominate the centres that were established within the care framework. The guarderías have until 2000 to meet the staffing and improved standards required by the 1990 Act. They can then apply to be recognised as approved early educational centres. Parents pay fees for day care settings.

EARLY CHILDHOOD EDUCATION

Some specifically pre-school educational settings are still operating under the terms of the 1970 legislation.

> ▶ The **escuelas de párvulos** are schools or pre-school units for children from three or four years to six. They may be attached to primary schools but some are independent units. These settings are the responsibility of the national Ministry of Education or the six autonomous communities that have a responsibility for education.
> ▶ The **centros preescolares** admit children from two years to six. These may be private settings or come under the responsibility of local authorities or those communities that do not have an educational remit.

Opening hours also vary but tend to follow the school hours including the long mid-day break lasting into the afternoon. Pre-school education is usually free but some centres offer additional hours and activities for which parents pay.

In terms of the 1990 Act these centres are within the early childhood framework of educación infantil and may be called **escuela de educación infantil** (school for early childhood education). In theory, the centres should offer provision from birth to six years in the two cycles (see page 163).

Provision can be more limited in the rural areas. Home visiting **(preescolar na casa)** educational services, seasonal groups or mobile provision are sometimes available through compensatory education programmes. Some rural and urban areas have access to the **casa de las ninõs**, centres for children (0–3 or 0–6) and their daily carers. These settings aim to offer an educational experience for children and social contact for parents and other carers.

NUMBERS OF CHILDREN

Following the expansion of early childhood provision, increasing numbers of Spanish children are in publicly funded centres. In 1993–4 almost half of three year olds (47.4%) were attending a nursery education programme. The majority of four year olds (99.4%) and 100% of five year olds were in pre-school provision.

Most of the provision for under threes is privately run and there are no reliable figures for these settings. It is estimated that private and publicly funded settings together offer provision for about 5% of the under threes, with lower levels of provision for under ones. The national statistics cover some wide regional differences. For instance, in 1993–4 the provision for two year olds varied between over 10% to less than 4% in some areas and for three year olds from more than 75% to less than 50%.

Family day care

This is not at all a common form of provision and such provision as exists is unregulated. There are no reliable statistics. Care within the family appears to be by far the most common option when no publicly funded provision is available in centres.

Family obligations and employment

In contrast with many other EU countries, Spain has a relatively low level of maternal employment. In 1996 35% of women with children under ten years were working, 29% in full-time jobs. The level of maternal employment in Spain is most similar to the low level in Ireland.

Spain has experienced periods of economic recession over the 1980s and 90s, during which unemployment as a whole has increased. The second half of the 1990s brought some increased prosperity and maternal employment in particular shows some regional variations. The financial cuts have affected many plans including the mid 1990s political aims of increased provision for under threes, more flexible school hours and parental leave. Spain offers a total of 36 months of combined maternity and parental leave, not necessarily paid and therefore it seems likely that the take up is low. Parents can reduce their working hours (unpaid) if they have children who are under six years or are disabled. Parents are entitled to two days paid leave for the beginning of a child's serious illness.

Statutory education

Primary schooling

Children start compulsory education in Spain at six years of age and the statutory system lasts until they are sixteen years. Schooling is free. The school day covers a morning and afternoon session and the hours vary between regions. The primary school holidays are eleven and a half weeks longer than the average annual leave for employed adults.

Out-of-school provision

Previously children have been expected to return home for the three hour mid-day break, but city schools in particular are more likely now to offer lunch and supervision over this period. In public schools the parents' associations usually organise the service and in private schools it is managed by the school's owners.

General out-of-school care is not a common form of provision and is unregulated. Workers in such services as exist are called **monitor** and there are no official training requirements. There is very limited term-time care, although holiday playschemes seem to be increasing in availability. The wide range of skills or recreation services are not organised to offer care and tend to operate more as courses for children to learn specific skills. Families who need childcare after school usually make private arrangements.

16
Sweden

National background

Geographical location

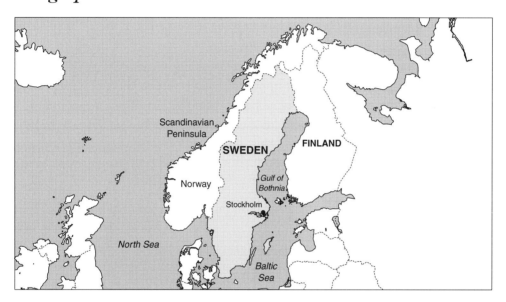

Sweden is a northern European country, sharing the Scandinavian Peninsula with Norway to the west. Sweden has another land border, with Finland in the north-east, and otherwise has coastal boundaries. A long coastline to the east joins the Gulf of Bothnia and the Baltic Sea. To the south-west is a shorter coastline along the Skaggerak and Kattegat straits that lead into the North Sea. There is a narrow strait, the Sound, separating Sweden from Denmark to the south.

Sweden is a relatively flat country, with the land sloping towards the mountains along the border with Norway. Half of its land surface is covered by forests, there are a considerable number of inland lakes and thousands of islands along the rocky coastline. The Gulf Stream provides Sweden with a milder climate that its northerly position would suggest.

Politics and government

The Kingdom of Sweden has a constitutional monarchy with a parliamentary system of democratic government. There has been a move towards decentralisation of organisational structures, with a delegation of responsibility to the 288 municipalities. Control of early childhood provision has been decentralised along with other services.

Sweden has remained neutral since the beginning of the nineteenth century and was uninvolved in both of the world wars of the twentieth century. The country's history of non-alignment has meant that Swedish people have often held major positions within the United Nations.

Swedish political policy has been to create a society in which there is a comprehensive pattern of family support measures. Early years childcare and education are part of a broader social policy and pattern of public spending that seeks actively to support families. Sweden also has an explicit policy to promote the rights of children and this perspective is far more reflected in legislation than in most other EU countries. Corporal punishment is banned by law and a Children's Ombudsman has the role of ensuring the implementation of the UN Convention on the Rights of the Child.

Social and economic framework

Historically Sweden has developed from a poor nation into a highly developed post-industrial society with an advanced welfare state. The economic recession of the 1990s placed the national system of universal social welfare under strain and some benefits have been cut or restricted. Sweden's average life expectancy and standard of living are amongst the highest in the world. Sweden joined the EU in 1995.

LANGUAGE

The population of the country mainly speaks Swedish, a language of Germanic origin in terms of the European family of languages. In the north, two minority ethnic groups speak other languages: the Finnish speaking population in the north-east and the Sami population, some of whom still live a nomadic lifestyle (see page 79).

POPULATION

In 1998 the population was 8.9 million, of whom 19% were under fifteen years of age, a figure that was 23% in 1950. During the 1980s and early 1990s Sweden's birth rate rose and in 1993 the country had one of the highest fertility rates in the EU (1.99). The relatively greater willingness to have children seemed to be influenced by the extensive services offered by the state to ease the private burden of raising children. However, the birth rate is declining once more.

About 5% of Sweden's labour force is foreign-born and of this group about 40% come from other Nordic countries, primarily Finland. Since the 1940s, Sweden has overall had a low birth rate, despite the temporary boost just mentioned. Over that time, immigration has accounted for about 40% of population growth.

Over the space of a few decades, Sweden has been transformed from a fairly homogenous society into one with considerably more diversity. Within the childcare settings more than 10% of children nationally have a non-Swedish family background but this part of the population is unevenly distributed so that some early years provision can have almost all the children with non-Swedish backgrounds.

URBAN-RURAL

The time of rapid economic growth after 1945 led to significant migration from the rural areas to the larger urban regions. The country communities became more sparsely populated and some government measures, including subsidies, were taken to counteract the shift.

Pre-school provision

The forms of early years provision in Sweden have evolved from three different traditions stretching from the nineteenth century. The early infant schools in the first half of that century were established with the aim of helping children from underprivileged families. The first day care centres also opened in the middle of the nineteenth century and continued to be mainly available for lone mothers until the 1960s. By the middle of that decade, the rise in maternal employment was creating pressure for an expansion in provision. A third strand, kindergartens based on the ideas of Froebel, were established at the beginning of the twentieth century.

Local involvement in the decentralised system

Following decentralisation, most of the local areas have set up committees to deal with issues relevant to children and adolescents in the region. Teachers and heads of the early childhood centres and out-of-school provision are members of the local committee. Decentralisation has brought some variety in standards for centres and the pressures of economic recession have raised concerns about quality. However, the standards of Swedish centres still appear to be high compared with many EU countries. Early years centres have a considerable amount of autonomy.

Since 1995 all the municipalities of Sweden have been obliged to offer a legal entitlement to childcare for parents who want to work or study from when their child is between one to twelve years of age. The legal entitlement is also for children of non-working parents when the child has special needs. The childcare sector used to be the responsibility of the welfare services. However, from 1997 all publicly funded services for children outside the compulsory school system were transferred from the Ministry of Social Welfare to the Ministry of Education.

Children start compulsory school at seven years, although schools have to take six year olds if their families request it. Currently many families prefer children to stay in their pre-school provision.

Population movements across Europe are often reflected in neighbourhoods – a high road in South London

Sweden takes a coordinated approach to early years provision and has set standards to aim for high quality, in particular through a high ratio of staff to children. The avowed objectives of all early years provision is to promote gender equality and social responsibility and to promote active bilingualism and bicultural identity in children from minority ethnic groups.

Early years provision

Sweden has a coordinated system of pre-school education and childcare. All the different types of provision are now under the responsibility of the Ministry of Education and local control. The general term **försköla** is used to cover provision within full and sessional day care centres and open drop-in provision.

Childcare centres are the responsibility of the municipal authorities. Services used to be supplied almost entirely by the local authorities but greater variety has been encouraged such that cooperative or private organisations can obtain public funding to develop provision. Parental cooperatives are the most common form of the more privately organised provision. Since 1991 private centres have increased in numbers, both in response to demand and to a government policy of increased parental choice. From 1995 municipalities are legally obliged to make childcare services available to parents on request without unreasonable delay.

FULL-DAY CENTRES

Daghem are full-day all-year-round centres for children from about one year of age to six years. Centres can take babies from birth but this is unusual, since Sweden gives favourable parental leave between mothers and fathers. In 1994 about 33% of under threes were attending publicly funded services and nearly three quarters of this group were in the centres. The remainder were in family day care (see page 175). Children in the centres are usually grouped into two sections: so-called sibling groupings of under threes and over threes. Centres vary and some have narrower age groupings than others.

The centres are staffed by **försköllarare** (early childhood educators) and **barnskötare** (nursery workers). The försköllarare have a three year training at a higher education institute or university and gain a degree in child and youth studies with a specialisation in early childhood education. The barnskötare have a three year training at the upper secondary level of school. All the vocational courses share some core modules and then students chose options, in this case one on childcare and leisure time studies.

Daghem are established to cater to children whose parents work or study and for children who need some kind of special support. Parents pay fees according to family income and the hours needed. The local authorities determine standards and ratios can be one adult to 3 to 5 children under three years and two to three and half adults for every 18 to 20 children from three to seven years.

PART-TIME PRE-SCHOOLING

The **deltidsgrupper** or **deltidsförsköla** are part-time nursery schools mainly for six year olds in their last year before compulsory schooling, although children can attend from four years. These centres are sometimes called **lekskola** (playschool). In 1994 most six year olds (98%) were attending the deltidsgruppper or early entry pilot classes in primary schools.

Attendance is free for six year olds and the settings tend to follow school hours and terms. There may be separate groups of morning and afternoon children. The usual ratio is 2:20 and one adult should be a förscöllarare. From 1998 it became compulsory for all municipalities to offer this type of pre-school class to six year olds, although attendance by the children is optional.

The groups are sometimes located within daghem but more often are separate centres with their own manager. The programme for children is similar to that of other children of the same age in the daghem and the deltidsgrupper are not focussed only on school preparation. They are staffed by förscöllarare and barnskötare.

Pre-primary schooling for six year olds only is called **sexårsverksamhet** and tends to be located in primary schools. Teachers and förscöllarare then work together with the group. The methods and grouping of the pre-primary class varies between schools and some merge the six year olds with early years of primary school. As this kind of provision grows, the deltidsgrupper seem to be declining in numbers.

In 1994 72% of the age group of three to seven years were attending publicly funded provision. Over three-quarters were in centres and the rest in family day care. Since that time, the pre-primary provision has increased and so the picture has probably changed.

DROP-IN FACILITIES

Öppen försköla are part-day drop-in centres for children from birth to six years and their parents, although there is no strict upper age limit for children. The centres operate to offer community contact and advice for parents whose children do not attend other forms of early childhood provision. The centres are also used by family day carers (see below). The centres are managed by a försköllarare and receive state funding. They have usually been established through a parents' initiative and in 1992 there were 1500 centres in Sweden.

Public funds supply the main source of finance for day care costs so that the cost to parents is less than some other EU countries, for instance the UK.

Local authorities are obligated to provide early years provision for disabled children if families request it and in most cases the children join the mainstream settings. Some settings offer specialist groups in which about half of the children have disabilities. Special units may sometimes address the needs of children with a particular disability such as deafness. Under specified conditions, disabled children are entitled to a personal assistant within their childcare setting or at home. Disabled older children either attend mainstream school or special school, if their disabilities are such that they cannot manage in main school.

Family day care

Familjedaghem (family day care) is usually the responsibility of the municipal authorities, although final arrangements are made between carers and the families. In 1994 about 12% of children from birth to six years and 8% of seven to nine years were with family day carers. The cost of the care is met jointly through central government, the local authorities and fees from parents (about 15% of the cost). The proportion of children in family day care declined with the increase in public day care provision in the centres.

The **dagbarnvårdare** or **dagmamma** (family day carers) used all to be state employees but it is now possible to be self-employed and receive a state subsidy. Family day carers are usually paid on the basis of caring for three or four full-time children but in practice they often care for between four and eight because some attend only part-time.

Carers are supposed to be trained through a local authority course but not all are. A three-family model now also exists in which carers are a qualified barnskötare who cares for the children of three families in one of the family homes. Most of the children in family day care are of pre-school age, especially the under threes, although this provision does cover school age children especially where there is limited local centre provision.

Family obligations and employment

In 1993 75% of Swedish women with children under ten years were employed, 40% on a part-time basis. Of women with children under seven years the overall percentage remained at 70% but the proportion working part-time was higher, at 53%. For instance, in 1993 70% of mothers of children of less than six years were working.

Most parents return to work after the end of their parental leave. Mothers on parental leave are still counted as employed and 87% of those with a baby under a year old are at home with their child. About a quarter of women with a child less than seven years are at home on parental leave in contrast with 5% of women whose children are between seven and ten years.

Since 1994 a parent has been entitled to stay at home with a child for a total of eighteen months paid parental leave. This time can be taken up until the child's eighth birthday in variable patterns. Parental leave can be taken by either parent, although it is taken more by mothers than fathers. Parents also have the legal right to work 75% of usual hours without loss of pay until their child reaches eight years. There are also additional days, paid at a proportion of earnings, to care for a sick child. Sweden therefore offers a total of 36 months of combined maternity and parental leave.

Statutory education

Primary schooling

Children start compulsory school at seven years, although there has been discussion about lowering the age to six years in line with many other EU countries. From 1997 all the municipalities are obliged to accept six year olds into primary school if their parents wish it. Compulsory education lasts for nine years, or until children are sixteen years and all schools are coeducational. Most schools are state run but there are some independent schools.

In the north of Sweden, Sami families are offered education in their home language, sometimes in a separate Sami school and sometimes within the mainstream. Sami educational facilities are also responsible for supporting children in an understanding of their Sami culture.

The school day lengthens as children get older. The pre-schooling year for six year olds and early years of primary school last for half a day. The difference between school holidays and the average annual leave for employed adults in Sweden is nine and half weeks.

Out-of-school provision

Out-of-school provision is known as **skolbarnsomsorg.** There was expansion of out-of-school care in the 1970s but not to the same extent as the early years provision.

From 1995 greater obligation was placed on the local authorities to provide out-of-school places for children of parents who were employed or studying and to make this available without unreasonable delay – much the same requirement as for pre-school day care. From 1997 this provision was also the responsibility of the Ministry of Education with the local authorities. Local authorities determine standards and the ratio is usually one adult to ten children.

In 1994 about 27% of six to twelve year olds were in out-of-school provision, most of the new places being taken by six and seven year olds. There are noticeable regional differences with less provision in more rural areas. Overall in 1994 there was national out-of-school provision for about 53% of the seven to nine year olds and less (about 5%) for the ten to twelve year olds, who were judged as a lower priority than younger children when provision was limited.

Until the mid-1980s the most common form of out-of-school provision was the **fritidshem** (literally free time home), a leisure centre that covered the hours before and after school including the provision of a mid-day meal, and the holidays. This kind of out-of-school provision used mainly to be run in separate centres that are regulated and run by specially trained staff. However, there has been a gradual move for some out-of-school provision to be located in primary schools themselves and the provision is then called **integrerad skola och friditshem**. Improved contact between out-of-school provision and the schools seems to be one reason, but economic concerns are also relevant. The school based services tend to be open only during term time.

The programme of the out-of-school facilities has much in common with that for the younger children. The aim is to support children's all-round development and to encourage them to take an active part in local community life. Parents pay fees for the service.

The out-of-school workers have their own, three year, university level training (the only kind in the EU at this level) and qualify as a **fritidspedagog** (literally a free time educator). They are assisted by barnskötare whose training extends to cover this age range.

Some afternoon youth clubs are also run for the ten to twelve year olds who cannot find a place in the out-of-school provision, which gives priority to the younger children when demand outstrips supply. There are no figures available on usage. The clubs are usually run by the local authorities but sometimes are organised by parents or a welfare organisation. They are also usually staffed by fritidspedagoger. Sometimes these flexible drop-in facilities are free and sometimes there is a charge.

17

The United Kingdom

National background

Geographical location

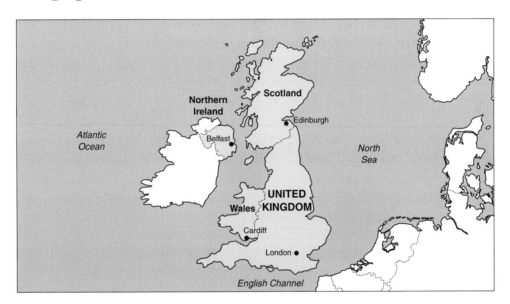

The full name is the United Kingdom of Great Britain and Northern Ireland, although UK is the usual shorthand. The UK is located off the north-western coast of mainland Europe and comprises most of the landmass known as the British Isles. The exception is the southern part of Ireland that has been a separate country since 1922 (see Chapter 10).

The four countries within the UK are therefore England, Wales, Scotland and Northern Ireland. The first three countries are part of the same island landmass, but Northern Ireland is part of a second island lying to the west and sharing a land border with Ireland. The UK is bounded by seas: the North Sea in the east, the English Channel in the south and the Atlantic Ocean in the west.

The UK also includes a number of smaller offshore islands. The island identity has been an important part of UK history (no part of the UK is further than 75 miles from one of the surrounding seas) and has contributed to a sense of being technically part of Europe, yet separate. An energetic maritime tradition, combined with imperialist expansion in previous centuries, led to a network of links to other parts of the world.

Politics and government

The UK has a constitutional monarchy with a parliamentary form of government. Central government has traditionally been in London, England but both Scotland and Northern Ireland, less so Wales, have long had some different and separate legislative structures and educational systems.

Up until the last decade of the twentieth century, the UK ran mainly as a political system centred on London but with a range of responsibilities delegated to local authorities in the different regions. Strong independence movements in Wales and Scotland led by the end of the 1990s towards a reorganisation of political and economic power called devolution. Some separate political structures have emerged for both Wales and Scotland and these include control and initiatives for childcare, early education and out-of-school care.

Northern Ireland has a different and troubled history characterised by religious divisions between two forms of Christianity: Catholic and Protestant. The religious divide has been interlocked with political, economic and social divisions in a national pattern known as sectarianism.

Social and economic framework

Immigration to the UK starting after the second world war and increasing through the following decades, often brought individuals and families from countries that had been part of the British Empire, which later become an international network known as The Commonwealth. These links, and a strong sense of historical association with the United States, led to an outlook from the UK that has not always been enthusiastically European. The many non-European international links also mean that the UK is not part of any obvious geographic block of western industrialised nations. The UK joined the EU in 1973 after some ten years of negotiations (see page 10).

The UK no longer occupies the position of major world power that it enjoyed into the first half of the twentieth century. It was one of the first

European countries to industrialise but many of the previously strong manufacturing industries have declined. Such changes have contributed to the significant differences between parts of the country and a national divide in which the south is noticeably more prosperous than the north. Although it has many areas of prosperity, the UK also has areas of social deprivation and poverty that are among the worst in Europe. As a whole the UK has a striking gap between the best and the worst off in its population.

LANGUAGE

The main and official language of the UK is English. However, many additional languages are spoken in different regions. These are from two broadly different sources:

▶ The Celtic languages of Welsh, Scottish Gaelic and Irish Gaelic have a very long, although disrupted, history in the UK. Promotion of the languages and of bilingualism has become a more active issue within early years and schools towards the last decades of the twentieth century.

▶ A range of languages are spoken by families who migrated to the UK within the twentieth century, mostly in the second half. Minority ethnic groups whose country of origin is not the UK are unequally distributed, so that diversity of culture, religion and language is far more prevalent in cities and urban, rather than town or rural areas.

POPULATION

In 1998 the population had reached 59.1 million of whom 19% were under fifteen years of age, a figure that was 22% in 1950.

URBAN-RURAL

In 1990 the overall population density was 235 people per square kilometre but this average included significant variations between a high average density of 871 people in north-west England to a low of 65 in Scotland, which has the most extensive and remote of the UK rural areas. Like some other EU countries, the UK has some areas classified as rural that are peri-urban, with some of the population commuting to their work.

Pre-school provision

General background

Organised care and early education developed in the UK during the late eighteenth century. Some early nineteenth century developments were particularly UK innovations, led by people like Robert Owen (see page 27) and David Stow. Nursery education as such developed along the lines promoted by European figures such as Froebel and Montessori. Margaret McMillan pioneered nursery schools in England, taking an approach that blended care and education, stressed learning through play and the value of the outdoors. McMillan was increasingly influenced by the ideas of Froebel.

Although the four countries of the UK share some themes in early years provision, each has some specific issues and the pattern of different kinds of provision varies considerably, also between regions within each country.

DIVERSITY IN PROVISION

Compared with many EU countries, the UK has a highly diverse and fragmented pattern of early years provision. The care and educational split is of long-standing and responsibility for the two parts has been divided both at national and local levels. Some local authorities and centres have worked hard to combine the two strands.

CHANGES IN THE 1990s

The early years provision experienced considerable change within the 1990s, partly through policies towards the end of the Conservative government and at an increased rate after Labour came back into power in 1997. Early years provision as a whole became a national and local priority and then the day care aspects were brought to the fore.

In the last years of the 1990s local authorities have been required to gather information and to extend their provision for pre-school education, childcare options and out-of-school care. The local Early Years Development and Childcare Partnerships (150 in England by mid-1999) have operated to very tight time schedules and regional differences are significant. Further initiatives, reviews and consultations have created a time of significant change in which it is too soon at the time of writing (1999) to identify a clear picture of the provision that will emerge. Diversity is likely to continue, both because of pre-existing regional differences and a laudable aim to respond to local needs.

Day care centres

Day care in the UK has developed through a diversity of provision. The patterns of responsibility for childcare provision are in the process of change.

Previously any care settings came under the national Department of Health and locally under Social Services. The provision has now effectively moved to the responsibility of education departments, nationally and locally. Settings have been registered and inspected under the Children Act 1989 with the regulations being followed by the local social services inspectorate. Changes proposed in 1999 mean that the educational inspectorate (OFSTED) looks likely to take over the whole regulation framework for young children.

LOCAL AUTHORITY DAY NURSERIES

State run **day nurseries** are available only on criteria of social need. Parents are unlikely to pay fees. Day nurseries have diversified in terms of the kind of provision, sometimes offering full-day, all-year-round care but increasingly offering sessional places and some level of parent involvement with a view to family support.

Some nurseries are called **children's centres** and some with a strong social work orientation are **family centres**. State day nurseries do not provide day care for working parents unless there is some defined social need. Probably about 1% of under fives attend the different types of local authority nursery. Slightly higher coverage may now be achieved by a shift towards more sessional places. Statistics can be confusing since figures for apparently day care provision can include local authority funded places for children in specialist pre-schools and playgroups, most of which are likely to be sessional.

COMBINED CENTRES

Since the 1970s a range of centres have developed that offer a blend of care and education and provide hours that may meet family's day care needs. Each centre tends to operate slightly differently as the management, funding and staff team work to bring together different systems. The combined centres are known by different names, including children's centres, nursery centres and other similar titles. These settings may be run by voluntary organisations or have some local authority funding. Some have become classified as **early excellence centres.** The aim is to have 25 such centres by 1999.

PRIVATE NURSERIES

During the 1990s there was a significant expansion in **private day nurseries**. Some are single businesses but more are part of small local businesses or substantial chains with up to 50 to 60 day nurseries across the country. Parents pay fees for private childcare.

Other nurseries

There are a small number of **workplace nurseries** where a company will organise a nursery, pay a specialist company to run the setting or buy in places in an existing nursery. Sometimes **community nurseries** are funded to serve a specific local catchment area.

Childcare fees are paid directly by parents. The fees may sometimes be subsidised in some way, but are largely met by the parents themselves. UK parents pay amongst the highest childcare costs in Europe, meeting more than 90% of the cost in 1996. (Data from the Family Policy Studies Centre.) The introduction of the Working Families Tax Credit will help some parents on low incomes who are using childcare provision registered under the Children Act 1989.

Ratios in the different kinds of early years settings have been set by local authorities in line with national government guidance. The ratios are usually 1:3 for children under two years, 1:4 for children between two to three years and 1:8 for three to five year olds. However, changes in 1999 indicate that settings who employ a nursery teacher may be allowed to increase the ratio for three and four year olds to 1:13.

The workforce

Day nurseries and the different kind of children's centres have a variety of qualified and unqualified staff. Day nurseries have largely moved away from the previous paramedical emphasis and staff are expected to be able to combine the care and early educational strands. Managers are most likely to have qualifications within early years care and education.

Nursery nurses (who may also be called nursery officers or early years workers) have completed training in early years care and education through two year courses usually taught at the tertiary education level. Nursery nurses can also work in nursery schools or classes and in the early years of the primary school in an assistant role to teachers.

In the late 1990s there has been an attempt to reorganise the confused state of early years training, with the additional aim to establish clear pathways between different kinds of practical work with children. A diversity of qualifications and training courses will continue for some time. Some are within the National Vocational Qualifications (NVQ) framework with courses run by a number of awarding bodies, such as CACHE (Council for Awards in Children's Care and Education) and EDEXCEL.

The first level of training is usually a two year course at a college of further education or sixth form college. In Scotland the Scottish Vocational Qualifications are awarded by SCOTVEC. In Northern Ireland childcare workers are trained to work with under fours through a diploma that takes about one year.

Children's centres that aim to bridge the care-education divide usually have some **nursery teachers** as part of the team. Family centres usually have a combination that includes some staff with **social work** training.

Family day care

Known as **childminding** in the UK, family day care has a long tradition of meeting the needs of working parents. Although there have been some schemes of childminders sponsored and paid for by the local authorities, the majority operate as self-employed carers and negotiate directly with parents. Local authority day care departments usually run a service for putting families in touch with registered childminders and have also sometimes run training.

Childminders are registered and inspected under the Children Act 1989. Childminders are usually limited to three children under five years including their own. Nannies who work with three or more families are judged to be operating like a childminder and also come under the Act. Otherwise the arrangement between family and nanny is regarded as a completely private arrangement. Childminders may receive training locally and the National Childminding Association (NCMA) works to offer training and promote quality in the service. A new possibility is that childminders may form networks to offer broad early years provision that would then be inspected under the OFSTED framework.

Family obligations and employment

In the UK day care, as opposed to early education, was linked completely with maternal employment. An impending labour shortage in the 1990s created a political interest in bringing more women, including mothers, into the labour market. This political change brought childcare onto the national agenda and led to local Partnerships being required to consider and plan for a childcare strategy.

Childcare has traditionally been viewed in the UK as a private matter to be organised between a family and provider. Official policy and pronouncements have often been negative towards working mothers. The increased profile of early years from the end of the 1990s has brought day care much more onto the political agenda. However, there is still considerable confusion and political spokespersons often talk of expansion of nursery education as a response to the childcare needs of working parents (the hours in no way fit).

In 1996 53% of mothers with under tens were working, the majority of the jobs being part-time. At this time the UK had one of the lowest rates of full-time working by mothers in the EU. However, in the ten years since 1985 the rate of maternal employment had increased significantly (in 1985 38% of mothers were working). Generally the rate of maternal employment in the UK increases with the age of the youngest child in the family.

In 1999 the Daycare Trust (*Childcare Now 1: the first steps*, May 1999) pointed to the most pressing childcare needs being for children under three years. The proportion of parents who decide to work is rising faster for parents of children under four than for parents of older children. 55% of mothers of children whose youngest child is under five years are economically active, although not necessarily full-time and two-thirds of mothers now return to work after maternity leave.

Active attempts and finally government support for expanding childcare has made a difference in the level of UK provision. The Daycare Trust (same publication as above) drew on DfEE statistics for 1997 and 1998 to show that over those years the level of provision for under eights increased. In 1997 there was one registered childcare place (childminder, day nursery or after school club registered under the Children Act 1989) for every nine children. In 1998 the ratio had become one place for every 7.5 children under eight years.

The UK has offered a combination of seven months of maternity plus parental leave, not necessarily paid. Having signed the EU Directive on Parental Leave, the UK must legislate for this particular development by the end of 1999. At the time of writing it looked possible that up to thirteen weeks of unpaid parental leave (separate from maternity leave) would be allowed to be taken up to the child's fifth birthday.

Playgroups

The **playgroup** movement developed in the UK during the 1960s as a parent-initiated response to the low levels of nursery education in many parts of the country. The movement had a strong philosophy of children learning through play and the value of parent involvement in the running of provision. The playgroup movement remained committed to partnership with parents but the groups do not insist on parent presence as volunteers in the groups.

During the 1990s a division within the movement led to two organisations. The main group was renamed the Pre-school Learning Alliance (and called their affiliated provision **pre-schools**). The Playgroup Network was established by members who felt the PLA was losing the play focus in an attempt to be more mainstream 'educational'. The Network continues to call their settings playgroups.

The playgroup movement has national organisations within the four countries of the UK and some settings within Wales, Scotland and Northern Ireland offer a bilingual form of provision (English with Welsh, Scottish or Irish Gaelic).

Pre-schools or playgroups are usually available to children from three to five years, although some will take children as young as two and half. During the 1990s many groups found that four year olds increasingly attended the reception class of the local primary school. Most groups are sessional and follow an opening pattern close to or shorter than local school terms. Some groups offer full-day provision and some have a specialist facility for disabled children. The pattern of provision does not provide childcare unless combined with other provision such as childminding.

Some groups have funding from the local authority but most have to undertake some fund raising themselves and parents usually pay a fee. The pre-schools and playgroups are usually staffed by **play leaders** who have attended training courses run by the relevant organisations.

The presentation of statistics in the UK makes estimates for any form of early years provision a complex matter. During the 1980s playgroups were the most common form of early years provision for three and four year olds and there were some estimates in the middle of the decade that about 40% of this age group attended playgroup. There have been significant changes during the 1990s and many playgroups have closed, having become financially non-viable when many four year olds were taken into reception classes. (See also the 1999 statistics about four year olds on page 190.)

Other forms of early years provision

Overall levels of services for young children are all lower in the rural areas of the UK. In some very rural areas playgroups and drop-in centres are the only form of early years provision. These settings do not claim to offer childcare but are often very welcome as the only available provision. Families can still travel many miles to reach settings that may only offer half day sessions.

Facilities for children and families also include a range of provision for which the aim is play opportunities for children and social contact for parents or carers. **Drop-in parent and toddler centres** are also known as one-o-clock clubs, because of their afternoon opening hours. Some rural areas are served by mobile provision with **playbuses**.

The late 1990s Sure Start programme has a focus on services for under threes and their families especially in disadvantaged or under-provided regions. The initiative may lead to local provision but it is too early to guess how much and of what kind.

The Bridgwater Children's Centre – combining care and early education

Early childhood education

The pre-primary form of education in the UK is called **nursery education**. This provision is optional and education does not become compulsory until five years of age. The level of provision varies between areas and is the responsibility of the national Department for Education and Employment and the local education departments. This provision includes:

▶ **Nursery classes** are the most common form of pre-school education. The classes are separate groups that are part of an existing primary school. The nursery class has its own room(s) and may also have a separate play area for the children. State nursery classes are free.
▶ **Nursery schools** which are separate centres with their own staff and buildings. Nursery schools may be state run, in which case they are free to parents or private in which case parents will pay fees.

Nursery educational settings are available for three and four year olds in England, Wales and Scotland and for two and three year olds in Northern Ireland, where the four year olds start statutory school. The publicly funded provision varies in quantity between regions. Attendance can be part-time or full-time (close to school hours) and some nursery schools and classes offer full-time places to the older children. Attendance is more often part-time in England and Wales, whereas provision in Scotland more often offers full-day places (school hours).

In 1996 about 26% of three and four year olds were in nursery schools and classes. Ratios in nursery classes or schools are respectively 2:26 and 2:20 where one adult is a nursery teacher and the second a nursery nurse.

Settings in the educational sphere in England and Wales, and any day nurseries or centres who want to obtain educational funding for their four year olds, have to develop a programme that addresses a required early years curriculum framework. The aims of the programme were initially defined through desirable learning outcomes, but a review has changed these into early learning goals to be achieved by children by the end of their first full year in primary school (by six years of age). Early years professionals continue to be concerned about the increasingly formal and adult-led nature of the early years curriculum as envisaged in the 1990s.

FOUR YEAR OLDS IN SCHOOL

In England there has been a pattern of early entry to school of four year olds. This trend started in the 1970s, especially in areas with a falling child population and increased significantly during the 1990s as a result of government schemes providing funds to settings for each four year old. A situation was allowed to develop in which a place in **reception class**, the first year of statutory school, was counted as a pre-school place. Although the official line was that parents had choice, the evidence has mounted that many felt obliged to accept early school entry to secure the primary school place.

In 1993 about 21% of three to four year olds were already in the reception classes of their local primary school. Department for Education and Employment figures in 1999 were that 56% of four year olds were in reception or infant classes in primary schools. This figure was presented as part of a total that 98% of four year olds were attending some form of early years or pre-school provision. However, when over half of the children are actually in statutory school the term 'pre-school' loses its accepted meaning. Something like 20% of the four year olds appeared to be in nursery class or school provision, about 15% attended private nursery, pre-school or playgroup and 5% were in independent schools. The figures appear to add up to more than 100%, which is symbolic of trying to obtain meaningful statistics in the UK!

The ratios in reception classes were set with the assumption that children are five years and over and can be as much as 1:30. Changes planned during 1999 mean that some local authorities may be able to apply for funding to bring the ratio more to 1:15. This government response has been in reaction to persistent criticism that four year olds in any genuinely pre-school setting experience considerably more favourable adult–child ratios.

The settings within the educational framework are staffed by **nursery teachers** who have completed a three or four year course at university level which equips them to teach children at the nursery or primary stage. In Northern Ireland teachers follow a course that allows them to teach the full age range of primary and secondary schooling.

Teachers are supported by **nursery nurses** who have one of the accredited early years qualifications (see page 184). The role of the nursery nurse varies considerably and depends a great deal on the outlook of the teacher who is in charge. In educational settings, the nursery nurses are usually called **nursery assistants**.

Statutory education

Primary schooling

Children start compulsory education at five years old in England, Scotland and Wales but a considerable number of four year olds are already attending primary school. The official starting age is four years old in Northern Ireland. Schools can be state (publicly funded) which are free to parents or independent schools (also called 'private' or confusingly 'public schools') for which parents pay fees. The state schools have to follow the National Curriculum and many independent schools also choose to follow this programme.

There are differences between the four nations in terms of state education:

▶ Wales has historically had least independence from central government in England although devolution may change matters (see page 180). Wales shares the same National Curriculum with England but with provision for Welsh as a language with equal status to English. To an extent, policy frameworks for early years services have been separate and sometimes key documents have been partly different in content and timing between Wales and England.

▶ Scotland's educational system differs from the rest of the UK in the naming of the different stages and in curriculum documents, both for statutory and pre-school provision.

▶ Northern Ireland has similarities in social and educational services to those of the rest of the UK. However, similar legislation has often been passed a few years later in Northern Ireland and practice reflects the divided society. Schools and pre-school provision usually exist in duplicated form within communities, with both Protestant and Catholic facilities. Integrated provision is a deliberate attempt to bring together children from families of the two Christian traditions and children from the small minority ethnic population.

The school day runs usually to mid-afternoon and, unlike many EU countries, children are supervised and can be fed a meal during the mid-day break from lessons. After-school provision is necessary for the hours before and after school and for the holidays. The difference between school holidays and the average annual leave for employed adults is eight weeks.

Out-of-school provision

The pattern of responsibility for out-of-school care has been varied. Local authority sports and leisure departments have sometimes taken the lead but voluntary organisations and the private sector have also offered provision. Under the Children Act 1989 any out-of-school provision with children younger than eight years has to be registered and inspected. Changes in the late 1990s make it likely that provision for older children will also be brought into a framework of regulation.

Out-of-school provision has been offered in different settings, not all of which have intended to meet family's childcare needs.

- Open access play settings such as adventure playgrounds or drop-in facilities are open to children, but the staff are not taking responsibility for them in a care approach.
- After school clubs and some holiday playschemes offer recreation and supervision for children. Clubs may operate on school premises or be in a separate building, in which case the club workers pick children up from named primary schools. This form of provision has been called **playcare** and there are divisions between workers who offer this service and others in the playwork movement who feel that it undermines the essence of children's freely chosen play.
- Some childminders take responsibility for children of school age for the hours they are not in school and the holidays.
- Some private nurseries and children's centres offer out-of-school provision, often to children who have attended the centre when younger.

During the 1990s there was a significant expansion of after school clubs, although the uncertainty of funding has meant that some do not last very long. Clubs usually cater to children from four years to about fourteen, although in practice clubs are more often attended by children of primary school age. The majority of clubs are in urban areas and rural areas face the twin difficulties of transport and lower numbers of children. After school clubs have been expanded both as a form of childcare and also in response to national government concern about unsupervised children being drawn into delinquency.

Many of the clubs are affiliated to the Kids' Clubs Network, a voluntary organisation with a long-standing commitment to out-of-school provision. By 1998 KCN had 4400 clubs on their database but they estimated that despite the growth in clubs, this form of provision could still offer places to only about 2% of 4 to 14 year olds. 1993 figures estimated that out-of-school provision as a whole was available to about 3% of five to fifteen year olds.

Out-of-school provision may be staffed by workers with a range of qualifications or none at all. The holiday playschemes in particular often employ young people with no specific training. Qualified **playworkers** may now have trained on a course providing the Playwork NVQ (SVQ in Scotland) qualification. Other training backgrounds may include Youth and Community worker.

Further resources

The suggested further resources include:

- ▶ Traditional style publications such as books, reports and articles.
- ▶ Internet websites which can be of especial use in cross-national research and data gathering. Some reports, both formal and more informal, are available on the internet.
- ▶ Useful organisations, some of whom are international and have their own website.

Although there are many useful written publications, this is a topic for which it is invaluable to become adept at using the internet.

Books

Dahlberg, Gunilla, **Moss**, Peter and **Pence**, Alan (1999) *Beyond quality in early childhood education and care: postmodern perspectives*. Falmer Press.

David, Tricia (ed) (1993) *Educational provision for our youngest children: European perspectives*. Paul Chapman.

David, Tricia (ed) (1998) *Researching early childhood education: European perspectives*. Paul Chapman.

Deven, Fred, **Inglis**, Sheila, **Moss**, Peter and **Petrie**, Pat (1998) 'State of the art review on the reconciliation of work and family life for men and women and the quality of care services'. DfEE Research Report RR44.

Melhuish, Edward and **Moss**, Peter (eds) (1991) *Day care for young children: international perspectives*. Routledge.

Moss, Peter (1992) 'Perspectives from Europe' in **Pugh**, Gillian (ed) *Contemporary issues in the early years*. Paul Chapman.

Oberhuemer, Pamela and **Ulich**, Michaela (1997) *Working with young children in Europe: provision and staff training*. Paul Chapman.

Owen, Charlie, **Cameron**, Claire and **Moss**, Peter (1998) *Men as workers in services for young children: issues of a mixed gender force*. Institute of Education Bedford Way Papers.

Penn, Helen (1997) *Comparing nurseries: staff and children in Italy, Spain and the UK*. Paul Chapman.

Rostgaard, Tine and **Fridberg**, Torben (1998*) Caring for children and older
   people: a comparison of European policies and practices.* Social Security in
   Europe 6: The Danish National Institute of Social Research 98:20

Publications of the European Commission Network on Childcare

This international network group ran from 1986 to 1996 and its full title is
European Commission Network on Childcare and other Measures to
Reconcile Employment and Family Responsibilities. The Network
published many valuable reports and these are worth seeking in your college
library or through other information sources. Please note that former
members of the Network do not hold copies for sale or loan. The reports
that I found especially useful include:

Network Team (1996) *A review of services for young children in the European
   Union 1990–95.*

Cohen, Bronwen (1995) *Childcare services for rural families: improving provision
   in the European Union.*

Jensen, Jytte Juul (1996) *Men as workers in childcare services.*

Meijvogel, Ria and **Petrie**, Pat (1996) *School-age childcare in the European Union.*

Magazines

These publications often have features relevant to a cross-national approach
or include reports of visits to the early years settings of other countries,
including EU members.

- ▶ *Child Education.*
- ▶ *Coordinate* (the house journal of the National Early Years Network).
- ▶ *Early Education* (newsletter of the organisation Early Education).
- ▶ *Nursery World* (the majority of useful articles that I have encountered
  for this topic were in this magazine over recent years).
- ▶ *Practical Pre-School.*

Journals

These publications are more focussed on broad practice issues and research.
Some can therefore be more academic in style, but nevertheless are worth
glancing through, if they are easily available in your library or resources
department.

▶ *Children and Society.*
▶ *Early Child Development and Care.*
▶ *Early Years.*
▶ *European Early Childhood Education Research Journal.*
▶ *International Journal of Early Years Education.*
▶ *International Journal of Early Childhood.*
▶ *IPA journal* (publication of the International Association of the Child's Right to Play).

Organisations, information centres and websites

Child Rights Information Network (CRIN)

A global network of organisations supporting effective information exchange about children and their rights, in general and under the UN Convention on the Rights of the Child. The Network is co-ordinated from Save the Children, 17 Grove Lane, London SE5 8RD Tel: 0207 703 5400 or contact them at the website:
http://www.crin.org/

Diversity in early childhood education and training (DECET)

This network brings together different centres and projects across Europe who share the aim of promoting cultural diversity in early childhood education. Contact the website at:
http://www.decet.org.

Early Childhood Unit, National Children's Bureau

A source of information and material, including European perspectives on early years. Contact the Library and Information Resource Centre, 8 Wakley Street, London EC1V 7QE Tel: 0207 843 6069.

European Early Childhood Education Research Association (EECERA)

This association promotes cross-national exchanges on research and on the links between research and practice in early years. The association is coordinated in the UK by Tony Bertram and Christine Pascal, who can be contacted at the Centre for Research in Early Childhood, Worcester

College of Higher Education, Henwick Grove, Worcester WR2 6AJ Tel. and fax: 01905 855068.

European Forum for Child Welfare (EFCW)

This forum is a regional group of the International Forum for Child Welfare that is a network of non-governmental organisations. The European group includes 27 countries. The Forum focusses on issues of children and safety within the family and the environment. The UK co-ordinator is Catriona Williams who can be contacted at Children in Wales, 25 Windsor Place, Cardiff CF1 3BZ Tel: 01222 342434 Fax: 01222 343134. Alternatively you can consult the Forum website on:
http://www.efcw.org

European Network for Children's Play (ENCP)

A network with the aims of linking people and organisations around Europe who are concerned about children's right to play.
Contact the website on:
http://www.ndo.be/encp

European Network for School Age Children (ENSAC)

This network began in 1986 and aims to develop awareness of care and recreation services for school age children and to promote cross-national exchange of ideas and experience. The Network now covers more than 20 countries and is coordinated in the UK by Pat Petrie at the Thomas Coram Research Unit, 27–8 Woburn Square, London WC1H 0AA Tel: 0207 612 6957. Or you can consult the Network website on:
http://home.swipnet.se/ENSAC

Eurydice

A substantial website that provides background information on early years education and some childcare for EU countries, with data up to the mid-1990s. The country profile reports include some historical background to the national systems. The website is:
http://www.eurydice.org

International Family Day Care Association (IFDCO)

A worldwide network of organisations involved in family day care (known as childminding in the UK). There are regional groups and the UK contact is Iris King, Sherwood, 2a Knock Road, Crieff, Perthshire PH7 4AH Tel: 01764 654367.

International Planned Parent Federation European Network

This information network provides facts and figures on population size, infant mortality and other national background data.
http://www.ippf.org/regions/europe./index/htm

National Play Information Centre

A source of information and material on play services and playwork, including a European perspective. Contact them at the 4th Floor, Dudley House, 36–38 Southampton Street, London WC2E 7HE Tel: 0207 240 9590, fax: 0207 240 8507 website:
http://www.npfa.co.uk

The European Commission Leonardo Project

The project gives funding for education and vocational training in Europe. Details are available from your area European Documentation Centre. You can ask your local library for details or access the information on the internet website:
http://europa.eu.int

The World Association of Childhood Educators

This is a non-governmental organisation, based in Spain, that encourages contacts and collaboration between early childhood educators. They will help to organise visits to other European countries. You can contact them at WAECE, Sede Central C/Averroes, 3 (Colonia del Retiro), 28007 Madrid-Espana. Tel 34 91 501 8754 or fax 34 91 501 8746 or consult their website on:
www.waece.com

Index

I have not used different national terms for workers or provision because these will mean little until you have read the relevant chapters. So, you will find 'day care centre' or 'out-of-school provision' followed by the pages that will direct you to this item for each country.